YOU GOT THIS!

HOW TO WIN AT COLLEGE

— BY —

JUHI KORE

You Got This
How To Win At College

First Edition

by Juhi Kore

Published 2018

ISBN 978-1-7327336-5-7

Cover Design: Marcel Sterk
Interior Design: YMMY
Editor: William Walls
Illustrator: Neelaja Phenany

Published by: Juhi LLC

Copyright © 2018 Juhi Kore. All rights reserved.

All rights reserved. No part of this work may be reproduced in any material form (including photocopying or storing in any medium by electronic means and whether or not transiently or incidentally to some other use of this publication) without the written permission of the copyright holder except in accordance with the provisions of the copyright, Designs and Patents Act 1988. Applications for the copyright holders written permission to reproduce any part of this publication should be addressed to the publishers.

Dedication

This book is dedicated to my one true non-human love, Tampa. Thank you Tampa for everything.

Acknowledgements

This book would not be possible without the support, prayers, and positive energy of some very important people in my life.

First and foremost, I would like to thank my parents for believing in my potential and helping me actualise my crazy dreams which included moving to the other side of the planet at 17 years of age. This book would truly not have come to fruition if you hadn't believed that I was deserving of the opportunity to study in America.

Second, I would like to express my immense gratitude and love for the University of Tampa, the University of Oxford, and my non-human love, Tampa. I would not be me without the experiences I have had because of you and for that, I am truly grateful. Thank you for providing me with the communities I have found myself to be a part of and thank you for making every day of my life so special.

A very big thank you to Jeff Gigante, my incredible mentor for always having my back and pushing me to accomplish every goal I ever mention to you.

Thank you to Peter Kageyama and Topher Morrison for writing books that have inspired me endlessly and for your constant support and guidance in this entire process. I would not have been able to do this without either of you.

Massive thanks to Jordan Huden, Kush Patel, Neelaja Phenany, William Walls, Eli Gonzalez, Alex Rodriguez, Joe Franzese, Gabriela Enache, Ayman Arandi, and Marcel Sterk for dedicating your time and energy to help make this book a reality.

Finally, thank you Brent Britton, Riddhima Khanna and my baby brother, Mihir and everyone else who has inspired me, educated me, and encouraged me. I love you all.

TABLE OF CONTENTS

Introduction 11
Who Is Juhi And Why Should You Listen To Her? 17
Pre-Flight Checklist 21
Part 1: Take Off 29
Chapter 1: Discovering Yourself And Your "Why" 31
Chapter 2: Accomplishing Your Goals 37
Chapter 3: Becoming A Great Communicator 49
Chapter 4: Becoming A Morning Person 57
Chapter 5: Taking Care Of Your Soul 61
Chapter 6: Taking Care Of Your Mind & Body 67
Part 2: In-Flight Navigation 79

Chapter 7: Adjusting To Your New Home..................81
Chapter 8: Making & Retaining Friends..................87
Chapter 9: Staying Safe..................93
Chapter 10: Addressing Safety Issues..................101
Chapter 11: Academic Success..................107
Chapter 12: Beyond Academics..................121

Part 3: Landing..................133
Chapter 13: Crafting A Professional Image..................135
Chapter 14: Building Your Personal Brand..................141
Chapter 15: The 4 Essential Elements..................149
Chapter 16: Networking..................163
Chapter 17: Launching Your Career..................171
Chapter 18: Finding Your Dream Job..................177

PSA For International Students..................189
Conclusion..................193
Research To Explore..................195
About The Author..................199

INTRODUCTION

Belief is a powerful tool. It can move mountains, cure diseases, and transform individuals. One of my strongest beliefs is that every single person has the potential for greatness. Now, I'm not saying that everyone will do great things by default, but I do believe that by discovering and utilising one's talent to its fullest, one has the capacity to do great things. I once gave a speech on this topic and focused on how grateful I am for my parents' belief in my potential. The thing is, I wasn't always the greatest kid growing up, and I certainly wasn't applying myself the way I should have been; but not once did my parents even consider the idea that I wasn't meant for great things. They internalised the belief that their daughter was going to accomplish big things; and although it took me a while to believe this for myself, I eventually did, and life took a wonderful turn.

The Purpose of This Book

It is not the purpose of this book to teach you how to get into university, and this book is most definitely not about cracking those awful standardised tests; the purpose of this book is to simply share my experiences, transformations, and key takeaways about how to succeed at university and in your life during university, because trust me, those two things, while very different, are equally important.

When I was initially trying to find a book about university, I realised that there weren't many on this topic at all. And of that small pool of books, there were maybe one or two that were from the student's perspective. The problem that I saw with these books was that you didn't actually get to know the student or develop a connection with them; they primarily consisted of just random quotes on random topics. The other books I found were written by a much older group of individuals and failed to relate to me as a young student. While the information made sense, I felt like I was being talked at, and not talked to, and once again, there was no real connection between the author and me.

Why Did I Write This?

I decided to write this book because I want to personally tell my story and inspire more students to attend university. I want to share the tips and tricks I learned and developed on how to succeed at university while working on my personal and professional development. I honestly wish I'd had a book like this to guide me through my university experience, because it's not easy. There are moments when you feel isolated and convinced that your problems are unique to you. But you know what? They're not. We all struggle with the same issues, and if I had known that, I would've spent fewer hours being mad at myself for not being relatable enough. This is why I want to offer you the opportunity to not feel alone. You have me and you have this community right here.

University IRL versus University in Pop Culture

I know for a fact that university is not easy. It's not all fun and games and it's not always as structured as you'd like it to be. It's nothing like high school; and most of all, it's not perpetual Spring Break, even if you're in Florida. I say the last part because it's a common misconception that I heard far too often at my own university; and sadly, those who come to college with that mentality are inevitably disgruntled with their college experience.

In my opinion, the misconception arises from the stereotypical party school portrayal of college life in pop culture. Movies, television shows, and even music videos give young kids the impression that their time at an American university will be filled with partying and booze, and that they can breeze through their classes with limited effort. Now, it is possible to live a life laden with partying and booze and yet finish college, but it is certainly not possible to do that and do exceptionally well in college, because there are only so many hours in a day and wasting precious time will not serve you well.

The Case for Liberal Arts

One of the major reasons that I chose the United States of America as my country of choice for college was the prevalence of the liberal arts system. In India, as well as in the United Kingdom and other countries, liberal arts programmes are not as popular. The education system in these places is slightly more restrictive in the sense that you are not learning much outside of the realm of your field. Now, to some people that might be more appealing because it takes less time (three years, ideally, versus four in the U.S.A.) and doesn't require you to take classes that are outside of your field; but if done correctly, you can finish your college degree in the United States in three years as well and receive a more holistic education.

Liberal arts is highly interdisciplinary, meaning, you will be required to take classes ranging from natural sciences and mathematics to social sciences and art in order to complete your degree. I believe that this helps one build a stronger and more open-minded worldview and gain skills through their education that are highly transferable.

In fact, Karen Abigail Williams, the director of admission at Eugene Lang College, The New School for Liberal Arts in New York says that, "[a] liberal arts education is more important than ever because with the recent economic downturn, we witnessed the decline (and, in some cases, the elimination) of several important industries, leaving highly skilled employees out of work in careers where job growth is not expected." This means that employers are actually seeking graduates with liberal arts degrees because this sort of education focuses on creating a culture of lifelong learning and critical thinking while ensuring that graduates possess diverse knowledge and skills.

Another aspect of liberal arts that I find very appealing is that it debunks the myth that some subjects are harder than others and that graduates of certain majors are more intelligent than those of other majors. This is especially true when it comes to the comparison between an engineering student versus a musical theatre student, because for some reason unbeknownst to me, engineering degrees are held to a very high standard, especially in the culture that I come from. By requiring all students to take classes ranging across various disciplines, it helps students not undermine others' educational paths, because as a Physics major, you might be doing great in your science classes but may experience a learning curve in a Psychology class, and vice-versa. This also helps students meet other students from many different majors, and hence, opens their minds up to many new worldviews.

Learning versus Studying

I have always been a curious person. I have always been the one to ask many questions in order to quench my thirst for knowledge. This is why I like academia; I like learning about new things and I felt like I learnt new things every single day during university, inside and outside of the classroom. What I do not like though, is studying and how the idea that studying is all-important has been reinforced in our minds. I think it is most important to learn, not to regurgitate information that you will forget after your exam. This is why I stress the importance of learning and enjoying what you learn because that is what makes the studying a little bit easier. The reason that I did not do well at all, during my school days was because I was studying about ten subjects and I enjoyed maybe three of them. But sadly, that wasn't enough and my overall performance suffered. My teachers did not care much because I was just a number to them and they did not try to engage us with the materials. Great things happen when students are able to enjoy what they learn, and this is why I am a huge advocate of everyone studying what their heart desires and not their parents' or friends' hearts.

Disclaimer

This entire book is purely based on my personal experiences with studying at a medium-sized private university in the United States of America and is filled with anecdotes of my peers from my university as well as at other universities. While the content has been acknowledged with approval by people from various backgrounds, there is no one-shot formula or one right way to do college and be successful, but I do believe that these practices will make you more likely to be successful at doing both. The research and data that I have included in this book has been indicated using footnotes wherever relevant, and I have made sure to include as much information as possible. Some of the content may be under more than one of the headings or categories because I believe it fits well in multiple areas and I would strongly advise you to make note of these things because it will be important to your overall success.

Education is a personal experience, and rightly so, because that's the beauty of it. You can have a great time and enjoy yourself while also being productive and learning a lot of cool things at university. This book will give you the tools to accomplish your goals and discover what the best way is for you to go through this experience and have the time of your life! Always remember, *you are greater than the highs and the lows.*

I am greater than the highs and lows - Juhi Kore

WHO IS JUHI AND WHY SHOULD YOU LISTEN TO HER?

So, why should you listen to me? What makes me the right person to give you all this advice about having the best time of your life at university?

Well, in the end you'll want to judge that for yourself, of course. But, I believe that I'm the right person for this job because I have already successfully walked the path. During my time at university, I completely transformed myself as an individual, created a whole new personal identity, discovered my life's purpose, and built meaningful relationships along the way, and thus, objectively speaking, I created a very successful experience for myself.

In addition to that, as someone who chose to study abroad for my overall university experience (in the United States of America) and then study abroad again, (in the United Kingdom), I was able to create systems and processes that I believed would help me be as successful in the U.K. as I had been in the U.S.; and by testing these first-hand, I can attest to their validity. But, I went a step further and coached several individuals in many of these areas and when I was able to watch them succeed in their own right, that showed me that my metrics were good enough for publication.

In my time at university, I also had the pleasure of serving as a mentor for first-year students. This meant that, during the three semesters that I held this position, I directly impacted the lives of close to 120 students and taught them most of the content that appears in sections two and three of this book while highlighting key ideas from section one.

Am I Really Qualified Though?

But wait... what makes me qualified to tell you about professional development? I mean, I'm just starting my professional career, right? Well, that's only partially accurate. I've actually been developing my professional brand and career since my first semester of university through my involvement with off-campus initiatives. I also served as a Career Ambassador at my university, which meant that I was trained to coach other students in all the areas that I talk about in section three of this book. In fact, for good measure, I've had all of that content approved by individuals who work in that department and I can thus assure you that it is the best first-step guide to building your professional life while still being a university student.

Finally, you can trust what I have to say when it comes to academic work as well as involvement because I graduated with the honour of magna cum laude, one of the highest honours that is bestowed upon undergraduate students at the University of Tampa, because of my 3.93 cumulative GPA. In addition to that, I studied abroad at the University of Oxford and scored the equivalent of an American 4.0 during my time there. In my three years of university, I was on the Dean's List every single semester while still being an award-winning active citizen at my educational institution and within the local community.

Now that you know a little bit about me, I would encourage you to reach out to me via email or social media and let me know how I can help you. As someone who deeply loved my university experience, I want to ensure that others are offered the same opportunity, and it is my honour to aid that mission.

PRE-FLIGHT CHECKLIST

Is University for You?

The first thing I want you to think about when you pick up this book, is whether or not an American university is for you. Now, don't get me wrong... I think anyone and everyone should get an American university education because it will change their life, but timing is critical. Besides, higher education is certainly not the only way to do well in life. I want you to really think about this because this book will add value to your life regardless of whether or not you pursue an American education. I just want to make sure you're not spending thousands of dollars if that's not something that will help you right now.

Is it for You Right Now?

One of my favourite quotes from the show, *How I Met Your Mother* is, "If you have chemistry, you only need one other thing. Timing. But timing's a b*tch."

This quote resonates with me on so many levels and I think it applies to more than just one's love life. If the timing isn't right, it's hard to reach a great level of success in whatever one may be trying to accomplish, regardless of one's potential. If you're only choosing to attend college because of external pressures, it's going to be a huge waste of your time, money, and energy.

In fact, a former student of mine was in exactly this situation. She was not particularly interested in college and she did her best to get into trouble as often as possible. In the end, she was expelled from the university for her bad behaviour. This is a perfect example of how one can ruin their chances at future success in higher education by making rash decisions with dire consequences during their teenage years.

In order to avoid jeopardising your future chances at ultimate success, it makes much more sense for you to take a gap year (or even many gap years) and go out into the real world and do other things and learn enriching lessons and then attend university with a newfound sense of appreciation for the experience.

Are You Meant To Attend University Right Now?

NO? Turn to page 17

YES? Turn to page 20

NO!

If you answered the question "Are you meant to attend an American university right now?" with a big fat "NO", there are many other things that you could do instead. I might be a strong advocate of a university-level education, but I still acknowledge that there are many other routes to success. I do not believe in the dichotomy of academic success and real-world success, because they coexist if you make them coexist.

I once met a man on an Amtrak (American railway service) train, and in conversation, he mentioned that he had never been to a university, but that he loved his job because it allowed him to travel extensively. As someone who measures success in terms of one's happiness quotient, I think this man is very successful in life. In this fashion, I'd like to give major shout-outs to lifetime entrepreneurs, vocational training institutes, MOOCs, community colleges, and the military.

Other Worthwhile Options to Consider

As I said, I am a strong advocate of a university-level education, but I understand that not everyone is mentally ready or prepared to go to college right out of high school. I believe that if one is truly disinterested in attending college after high school, they can choose other options to become productive human beings and gain valuable skills that will help them succeed in the real world.

For example, someone can choose to go to a vocational training institute and learn the tricks of a specific trade that interests them, then go out into the real world and apply that trade professionally. A study reported by the Technical and Vocational Education and Training United Kingdom (TVUTEK) found that 98 percent of people agreed that a vocational education is vital for other people's kids.

This shows that people are overwhelmingly in support of vocational training but need to personally partake in following this path.

A friend of mine, Rosa, elected to take the entrepreneurial route after high school and her drive and passion paid off monetarily because her business was generating a couple million dollars before she turned 21. She attended university later on in life and took classes that interested her and had a great experience with that. She did not finish her degree but has been an entrepreneur her whole life and in that regard, has been quite successful.

Another great way to dip your toes into academia without committing thousands of dollars to the effort is to enrol at a local community college. By doing this, you can get a good feel for the kind of environment higher education creates, and in the process, figure out if this is the path you want to commit to at this time. This is a highly beneficial approach if your interest levels and uncertainty levels are both rather high.

A friend of mine, Joshua, took classes at a community college for two years and got all his general requirement classes out of the way and is now on track to graduate in just two years at a four-year university. For him, this was a great way to save money while working full time and paying far less to take college-level classes that would satisfy the general requirements for any major that he chose, which helped him to offset the cost of his education even further.

In fact, if you're still in high school and thinking about college, please enrol in International Baccalaureate (IB) or Advanced Placement (AP) classes, because they will help you advance through university faster without compromising the knowledge gain. You'll earn college credit for the classes you've already taken in high school, and these will often fulfil general requirements, leaving you with the freedom to take classes in your major once you get to college. Because I studied IB for high school, I entered university with 24 credits and was on track to graduate a semester early. By taking just two extra classes during my first summer at the University of Tampa, I was able to graduate an entire year earlier than my fellow freshmen.

As for American citizens, another great way to offset the costs for your higher education while gaining real life skills, is to spend a few years in the military. If you have a strong sense of patriotism and feel like the civic duty of serving your country is your calling, you should pursue this opportunity. This will give you access to free tuition once you are discharged through "The Servicemen's Readjustment Act of 1944", popularly known as the G.I. Bill, especially if you are interested in getting a university-level education, but do not have access to the kinds of funds that are required to make it happen.

You can even consider using a combination of all of these to save yourself some time and money while giving yourself the best chance for success at university and in life. I know people who served in the Marine Corps and took classes during deployment or went to community college before deployment and then used their G.I. Bill funds to pay for university afterwards.

I believe that the bottom line is to take action and be productive. Learning is the most important thing you can do for yourself, regardless of what kind of learning you choose. And besides, even if you don't want to attend university at the moment, as someone right out of high school or in your early twenties, you can still use the personal development and professional development sections of this book, because all of that content is from the perspective of a young nerd bird spreading her wings and learning to fly.

YES!

If you answered the question, "Are you meant to attend an American university right now?" with a "Heck, yeah!", an "Absolutely!", or any other variations of this emotion, this book is going to be your best friend.

Unconventional Advice

One major piece of advice that I will give you right now, though (which might sound a little crazy, but trust me, it works), is that you need to have as much fun as possible during the summer before college. This will serve multiple purposes, the most important one is getting the whole "party mindset" out of your system. I can honestly tell you that the summer before I started university was my most unproductive summer ever, and that was the best thing I could have done for myself, because by the end of that summer I was so tired of partying and going out and being a crazy kid, that when it was time to start classes, I was ready to be productive while my peers were only beginning to experience some sort of freedom to be crazy kids.

In the United States especially, kids tend to feel suffocated in high school with all the school work, the rules etc. and when university comes around, they start to develop this new-found sense of freedom that makes them want to go crazy. There's also something oddly satisfying about finally being away from your parents and not having to follow their rules or telling them about your every move, and this can especially affect international students.

What You Need

Now let's talk about what you need to bring with you. And no, you do not need to bring your entire room from home. Along with your admission packet, you will most likely receive a list that the university deems as being a sort of "essential items" list that they think you should bring. It's important to look at this list and strongly consider following it because every university has its own rules as to what you CANNOT bring.

For example, at the University of Tampa, we were not allowed to bring any candles, incense sticks, or toaster ovens. It's also important to consider the weather where your university is located because that will dictate a lot of your clothing and footwear choices, among other things. Another reason that they provide you with that list is to make sure that you don't forget the small things. Pinterest was my favourite tool when deciding what I wanted to bring with me because there are so many inspiration boards that you can follow while designing your room. While I don't suggest bringing all your décor with you from home, you can certainly make a list of things that you want and either purchase them online and have them delivered to your campus or buy them locally at a Walmart or Target near your university.

I should also mention that you don't have to alter your daily routine extensively. If you use certain products on a daily basis, they might not be as readily available where your university is located, so feel free to stock up on those items. And one last thing: use the company that your university suggests for bedding and other similar items. This will be your best bet for fitting the bed size because big brand stores don't always make items that are a perfect fit. In my freshman year, I had friends who purchased their bedding at retail stores but had to return them when the size didn't match the beds that the university provided.

Other things that don't fall exactly under "What to Pack:" a mini refrigerator and a microwave. In my opinion, these are absolutely essential because they save time and serve well on lazy days. As to how you can come to be in possession of these, you have some options. You can either buy both yourself and then figure out where to keep them during breaks or if you move off campus. Or, you could coordinate with your roommate and each of you could buy one of the two.

During my freshman year, my roommate and I did this, and when I subsequently moved out, we simply chose what we each wanted to keep (we had gone halfsies on both) and it all worked out rather well. The reality is that dorm rooms are tiny and cluttering them with two or three individual sets of microwaves, mini refrigerators etc. is only going to make the space seem even smaller. It's much easier to buy things later if you feel like you need them versus trying to get rid of or sell stuff that you later discover you don't need.

Social Adjustments

When you get to university, you're going to make tons of new friends and meet many great people. That being said, it's important that you don't lose touch with important people from your "past life." If you do miss home, talking to people back there is the best way to make yourself feel better and less homesick. Besides, these are quite likely individuals who have known you for a long time and will be great judges for admiring your growth and development as an individual. On the flip side, they could hold you back if you try to tread extensively on undesirable paths.

Once I started being more active on social media about my involvements and accomplishments, many people from my "past life" reached out to congratulate me on my growth. These were people who had known me for 15 years, and not once had it crossed their minds that I might amount to anything out of the ordinary. The feeling of accomplishment that overcame me when these people told me they were proud of me and happy for me was like nothing else.

Part 1

TAKE OFF

CHAPTER 1

DISCOVERING YOURSELF AND YOUR "WHY"

In order for you to engage in personal development, you must first understand who you are as a person. What I mean by this is that you need to figure out how your brain works, how your emotions work, what your dreams and goals and aspirations are, what you are afraid of… you get the point. Simply put, YOU NEED TO KNOW YOU.

Personality Tests

One way to do this is through the administering of personality tests. Some tests that have proven extremely effective for me in my personal life are the Myers-Briggs Type Indicator

(MBTI), 5 Love Languages, Emotional Intelligence, Strengths Finder 2.0, DISC, and Emotional Agility tests. I took most of these during my introductory class for my Leadership minor, and others were either suggested to me or I found them online. I will provide you with a slightly longer description of my top three tests, but I do highly recommend taking all of the aforementioned tests because the analyses that they have provided me with are invaluable. I love taking personality tests online, but most of the other tests I have taken were for fun and were more *pop-psychology-ish* versus being credible indicators of my personality.

The Myers-Briggs Type Indicator (MBTI)

I would say that the MBTI has been very influential in my life, and although I originally took the written version that the university paid for, there is a great online version that will not only tell you your personality type but will also give you a detailed analysis about the type. One thing to remember about this one though, is that your type might change, because, more often than not, the circumstances that you are dealing with while taking a test like this one will have an influence on the answers you pick. It won't be drastically different, but one of your four letters might change.

For example, I switch between an ENTJ and an ENTP depending on the situation, but I would say I am an ENTP about 60 percent of the time. Another friend of mine reported the same type of fluctuation, but he switches between an ENFT and an ENFJ. So, don't be alarmed if that happens with you as well.

The Five Love Languages

The second test that I really do believe in, is the Five Love Languages test which was suggested to me by a friend. This test actually has two versions when you take it for yourself – "Single" and "In a Relationship," and your resulting languages can be wildly different in both scenarios. From what I have observed, the "Single" test gives you an analysis of how you communicate with friends, family, acquaintances etc. but the "In a Relationship" test is solely focused on how you best communicate with your partner. My results for both were rather different, but Words of Affirmation was a top score for me in both tests. I highly recommend doing both regardless of whether or not you are in a relationship because it helps you understand how you like to receive and show your love for a person.

For example, if your #1 love language is Quality Time, you are someone who enjoys spending time with your friends or your significant other and this is how you feel loved by them. If your #1 love language is Receiving Gifts, then spending time might not mean much to you, but if someone gives you small gifts, that is what makes you feel loved. It might also help to get your close friends or your partner to take this test so as to improve communication between themselves and you.

Emotional Quotient (EQ)

The third test that I want to talk about is another one that I learned about through my Leadership class. We were assigned the book *Emotional Intelligence 2.0* and the book was accompanied by a complimentary passcode to the Emotional Intelligence Appraisal test. The book and the test were both very good. The book provides a great background and an in-depth understanding of the concept of emotional intelligence and how you can use it to your advantage. The test shows you where your Emotional Quotient (EQ) level lies and what that means for you in your life.

The four main areas of EQ are: self-awareness, self-management, social awareness, and relationship management. While my understanding of this concept if through the lens of leadership, you can use it for whatever you would like.

There are other tests I've taken and can recommend. The Emotional Agility Quiz by Susan David, Ph.D., is a good all-around assessment of emotional strength and resilience that strives to apply equally well to both life and career skills. The CliftonStrengths Assessment (formerly known as the StrengthsFinder Quiz), is a bold attempt to parlay an assessment of personal strengths and weaknesses into a programme for self-improvement. The DISC Assessment has become nearly as well-known as Myers-Briggs in professional circles. DISC provides insight into how a person's self-image and natural traits influence the way they interact with people and their environment.

Personality tests are by no means an end all be all way of knowing yourself, but I do believe that they are a good place to start. This is especially true for students because time and resources might be limited. It's just not possible for all students to take time off from university and/or their jobs to go explore the world and "find themselves," so these tools can allow them to accomplish the same from the comfort of their dorm room. Oh, and if you come across any other tests that you deem valuable and recommendable, feel free to reach out to me and let me know about them because I would love to try them out!

Element "Why"

Imagine waking up every single day and not knowing what you stand for, or if you even stand for anything at all. If this describes you, does the idea of a higher purpose for your life feel so foreign to you that you live a monotonous routine every single day and don't even expect your life to change? If you're not taking action in any avenue of your life, why *would* your life change? The most detrimental thing to your potential, though, is not the "not taking action" part, it's not knowing why you should in the first place.

In order to achieve high levels of success, it's imperative that you have a strong enough reason for doing what you do. Does this thing you want to pursue help you wake up with a smile on your face every morning and go to sleep knowing that you're doing the right thing for yourself? If not, give it up already. If there's too much friction in some area of your life, more likely than not, it's a sign that you need to change it. That friction is God's (and the universe's) way of letting you know that you're not on the right track. I'm not suggesting that things aren't going to be hard when you're pursuing your dreams and fulfilling your purpose; what I'm saying is that there won't be as much of the sort of friction in your life that makes you feel unsatisfied with the course your life is taking.

The fact is, some people who live purposeful lives are fulfilled just by the fact of having discovered their purpose and living it, regardless of whether or not their work yields the massive monetary results that others might value. We're talking life priorities here. If monetary success is your priority, you won't be fulfilled if you don't achieve it, and there's nothing wrong with that. In terms of university, if getting an A is your goal, you might find yourself taking classes that are easier to score that A in; but if your goal is to maximise learning, you'll challenge yourself to take tougher classes. Neither of these approaches are right or wrong, they simply reflect different priorities.

Knowing your why can lead to a more fulfilled life because it allows you to only take on the things that align with your purpose. It also helps you fight the hard fights because you can see the bigger picture and know that it will be worth it in the end.

I personally find it excruciatingly hard to accomplish a goal if I don't have a bigger reason for doing it other than "I want to" or "I need to." That indispensable sense of urgency is missing. And when it's missing, it's almost impossible for me to get it done. For example, writing this book was really hard! But I knew that I had a bigger reason than just wanting to write this book. The bigger reason was you: the reader I hope to impact and inspire.

Chapter 2

ACCOMPLISHING YOUR GOALS

A popular notion in today's society is the idea of striving endlessly to make yourself better at your weaknesses. I'm a firm believer that doing so will only result in frustration. I believe that one must find one's strengths and then get even better at them. Doing so will propel you towards greater amounts of success because your mind and your body are already aligned towards this particular skill set. For example, if you are good at sports and not so good at singing, you will have to work much harder than someone who is predisposed towards being a good singer to achieve massive success in that field.

My friend Auro and I talk about this often. He's an all-star football (soccer) player at his university and has been pursuing this sport since he was very young. We went to the same school growing up, and everyone knew him as the best football player in that school because he played for the school, the state, and even the country. He moved to the United States when he was 15 to play for a club in the northeast. Yet, he tells me how awesome it is that I'm constantly involved with different things, and I tell him that I wish I had his focus because there are days where I feel overwhelmed by the chaos that is my life. I mean, the guy is going to be a professional football player and that has been his life goal since forever! We may not have the same life path, but what we completely agree on though is the sheer importance of following your passions and pursuing your strengths, because those two factors are so important to your success whether you're pursuing one thing or multiple things.

Finding Your Strengths

The first step to being successful in something is knowing what that something is. In my experience, a simple way to find your "something" is to take a piece of paper and a pen and write down everything that interests you AND that you're fairly good at. Once you have a list of those things, start going through that list, grouping things that are of a similar nature and labelling them accordingly.

The first (and most impactful) time I did this was when I was at a conference listening to a talk about pursuing your passions. The speaker was talking about the importance of finding your ONE THING and pursuing it, but I knew that I was wired differently and that I couldn't pick just one specific thing. I have a wide variety of interests and a large skill set. That, combined with my drive and my ability to grasp things fairly quickly, helps me pursue multiple things simultaneously.

So, I sat there and started writing. I came up with about 25 things that I felt interested in and that I was also fairly good at. I narrowed that down to about 11 things and then sorted those into three main categories. That's how I was able to identify my top three passions: public speaking, social entrepreneurship, and international relations. And ever since, if an opportunity is presented to me but it doesn't fall into one of those three categories, no matter how appealing, I will say no. I know that these are my top three interests, passions, and strengths, and that doing something else will not yield as much success in my life as these will.

The flip side of this activity is to write down everything that interests you but you either know only a little or nothing about it, but that you would love to explore further. Again, narrow these down to your top 3-5 things, and then every time you feel like procrastinating (let's be real, we all have those days), instead of looking for something else to occupy your time, you can pick something from this list and learn about it or practice doing it. This list can be as broad and as wild as quantum physics, calligraphy, and types of clouds (these are actually on my list)! But every time you catch yourself giving your time, energy, or attention to anything else, you'll want to reprimand yourself to keep yourself focused.

The Dreaded "Comfort Zone"

I want to emphasise the importance of trying new things and getting out of your comfort zone. If you're trying to develop that first list but are getting nowhere because there's just so much out there that you don't know, don't fret! Just make a list of things that interest you and that you want to try, and then actually go out and try them all! Without understanding where your passion lies and what your big WHY is, there is no point in pursuing a career or profession, because no matter how much monetary success you achieve, you'll never feel truly fulfilled or inspired by yourself or your work.

Two of my friends, who were business partners with one another, were doing rather well financially, but were both unsatisfied with their work. They were comfortable, but highly unsatisfied; and after recognising this in their personal lives, they realised that they needed to make a change. They were able to talk it through and create a workable situation for their business and for each other, while giving themselves the opportunity and the ability to pursue what they truly wanted to do outside of that company. That's another way of dealing with the comfort zone; you don't necessarily have to go all out. You can start dipping your toes into a new venture while retaining the profits or benefits of the one within your comfort zone.

It's the same with classes; if you don't enjoy your major and the classes you take, you won't feel like attending class or studying when you really need to. When I started university, I had almost no experience with public speaking, entrepreneurship or even international relations. I vaguely knew that I liked being in front of people, being my own boss, and learning about the world. And, if I hadn't taken a chance on myself and gone out of my way to experiment with those things, I would have never realised how much they actually mean to me.

The best example I can think of from my personal life is that when I initially started pursuing public speaking, I would sometimes be required to film myself and listen to it. And I HATED IT!!! Being my harshest critic, I would find so many faults in my voice, my stance, my words, just about everything! And now? I have a Facebook Live show where I make videos of myself talking ALL THE TIME! In fact, what I hated most was the sound of my voice when it was recorded, and now I have a podcast where all I do is record my own voice reciting poetry! Once you dissociate the fears and insecurities that you may have associated with a certain activity, it gets much easier to enjoy yourself and sometimes even fall in love with the activity itself! And it's not as if one day a flip just switched. As I was involved with our TV organisation on campus, I continued watching my recorded speeches. Finally, I found my bigger "why" for pursuing video, which was that I can't possibly be in front of everyone I want to impact from all over the world, but my videos do have the ability to reach anyone, anywhere. And that is how I started my journey on video.

University is the best time of your life to take risks, to try new things and to experiment. You're still young and energetic, still free from most of the adult responsibilities that older adults in your life have to deal with. If you want to dance but don't have the time to join a dancing club, take a dance class for academic purposes! Not only will you be able to try something that you've always wanted to try, but you'll also get credit for it! There are lots of other hacks that you'll discover throughout this book that will allow you to maximise your college experience to the fullest.

Don't Just Be Busy – Be Productive

A question that often pops up in my mind is "Why do I procrastinate?" This often results in me having a conversation with myself where I reply, "Because everyone procrastinates!" This will inevitably be followed by, "But, why do people procrastinate?" Finally, one day, this internal conversation resulted in me looking the question up on Google and coming across the research done by Joseph Ferrari, Ph.D., associate professor of psychology at DePaul University in Chicago. His research work focuses on procrastination. One of his highly-quoted findings is the identification of the three basic types of procrastinators: thrill-seekers, avoiders, and the indecisive.

The first type of procrastinators are those who enjoy the euphoric rush that comes with working against a tight deadline. The second, are those who avoid doing the task at hand because they're afraid; either they're afraid of failing because they care too much about what other people think of them or they're afraid of succeeding because they're afraid of taking on new responsibilities and other people expecting too much from them. And finally, the third type are those who want to absolve themselves of responsibility for the outcome of the task and will therefore put off making any decisions.

Dr. Ferrari also administered a survey that found 20 percent of the American population to be chronic procrastinators, but a meta-analysis by Piers Steel, Ph.D., from University of Calgary found that 80 to 95 percent of college students indulge in procrastination. This presents a big problem. The culture in most colleges and universities is that of procrastination. I personally identify as a procrastinator and I am quite certain that I fall into the first category outlined by Dr. Ferrari. And yet, being a part of this overwhelming majority doesn't inhibit me from accomplishing my goals. So, how do I manage to be an overachieving procrastinator? The three big things that have helped me are these: staying organised, setting goals, and having accountability partners.

Being Organised Doesn't Just Happen – It Takes a Plan

When I was younger, I would often create these large (and highly unrealistic) plans for myself that I intended to accomplish sometimes in the day, the year, or (on one occasion), my whole life. Yes, it's true. One time, my friend and I outlined our entire lives because we thought we knew exactly what was going to happen in our futures. But, I digress. More on that later. What I learnt in university, though, is that people are unpredictable because life happens. What I mean by that is, you can plan as much in advance as you like, but sometimes things might come up in your life or in other people's lives that might render all your plans futile.

A prime example of this from my own life was when I had all these interviews lined up for my #JuhiApproved Facebook Live Show right before I was leaving to study abroad at Oxford because I wanted to create as much content as I could in Tampa before my departure. But unfortunately, this was also the time that the United States of America faced one of the biggest hurricanes it had ever seen, and while most of the projections leading up to the hurricane stated that it would go through the east coast of Florida, the last few projections for the hurricane ended up showing that it was going right over Tampa and the uncertainty leading up to this hurricane inevitably cancelled a few of my shows. I then faced two choices: either give up and resume creating content once I was at Oxford or reschedule as many of the interviews as I could and finish strong. I chose the latter even though it was chaotic. My plan had certainly not gone the way it should have.

And yet, I also learnt that having a plan is quintessential. Mostly because having those interviews set up in advance meant that when people were back to their normal lives after the hurricane interruption, I was already on their to-do lists. So, every single one of my interviewees rescheduled for me and ensured that they were on my show.

Planning Fundamentals

Planning is important, and thus by association, planners become important. While there is no one planner that suits every single person's needs, there are some common types of planners that most people find useful. Personally, I like a specific planner from a company called ban.do® which has monthly and weekly spreads. While the cute quotes and stickers provide an interesting aesthetic, they aren't as attractive or useful to me. Also, this planner is quite large. But, it fits my needs and I like it a lot. Some people prefer smaller notepad-type planners and others need massive calendars. To each his own. One key thing, though, is to have at least two to three different points of reinforcement so that your tasks and goals are visible to you in multiple places at any given time, thus branding it into memory.

For example, when I use my planner to plan out my day I use a Post-it note with keywords for my tasks and goals and I use Google Calendar to have access to the same information on my phone. This makes it much harder for me to ignore my responsibilities thus ensuring that I accomplish my goals and CRUSH IT! Another system that I use for staying organised is Bullet Journaling, but due to its sheer importance and influence on my life, I discuss this more in detail later.

Successful Goal-setting

While planning your day, week, month, or even your life is great, there needs to be a system in place to ensure that you're meeting all those plans. Like with planners, there are many goal-setting systems available, and nearly all of them can be customised to suit your needs. I use my Bullet Journal to outline my yearly and monthly goals and my planner and post-it notes for my daily goals. But the system that I follow for setting those goals is the SMART goals system, and I outline my HOW and WHY for each of my goals, especially the big-picture goals.

The SMART goals system was first introduced in 1981 by George T. Doran in the November issue of the *Management Review* journal. While each letter can mean something different depending on the author you are referencing, a common version is:

> S for Specific
> M for Measurable
> A for Ambitious
> R for Realistic
> T for Time-bound

A good example of a SMART goal is something like:

- Reach out to two new mental health entrepreneurs in the Seattle area via LinkedIn for the next month.

This is specific, as I have listed who I want to reach out to, how, and where. It is measurable, because I know the number of people I want to reach out to in order to accomplish this goal. It is ambitious and yet realistic while being time-bound by stating exactly how long I want this goal to last.

Once I successfully create a goal using this metric, I will make sure I develop a HOW and a WHY for my goal.

Keeping the same example, a HOW would be creating a list of these potential people by researching mental health organisations in this specific city, and a good WHY would be because I am either working on a business idea or a research project in the mental health area and want to meet people who are active in this community in a specific city.

A study conducted by The American Society of Training and Development on accountability found that the probability of someone completing a goal if they have a specific accountability appointment with a person they have committed to is 95 percent as compared to a mere 10 percent if they simply have an idea or goal, so I am a staunch believer in the power of accountability partners.

Your accountability partner can be anyone from your parents to your mentor, but a really great accountability partner will be someone who is working on the same goal as you.

When I first became a morning person, waking up at 5:30am was not the easiest thing to do every single day. I soon realised that I needed more than just myself to hold me accountable and I started looking for friends who would want to join me in accomplishing this goal. Finally, my friend Ryan stepped up and said that he would join me on a morning walk every single morning. There is a beautiful waterfront road in Tampa called Bayshore Boulevard and we would alternate between going there or going to the Riverwalk every single morning to watch the sunrise and get our exercise in. This way, we were both able to accomplish our goal and had a buddy to help with the process. The flip side of this, though, is that sometimes, if one of you don't feel up to it, the other one may also drop out. This is why you need to find someone strong-willed as your accountability partner and both of you need to commit to really accomplishing whatever the goal is that you have set for yourselves.

The Magic "Bullet"

As a young girl, I repeatedly tried my hand at maintaining a diary. Sometimes, I'd manage to keep it up for a few months and sometimes only a few days. I even had the occasional 'mean boys reading my diary at school' drama. Finally, I decided that it just wasn't for me. So, I went through almost all of high school without a "diary." But all of that changed in March 2013 when I was introduced to the magical world of Bullet Journaling®!

To be honest, I don't remember how or where I saw it first, but I do remember watching the official video on Bullet Journaling on YouTube. I was so impressed by this unique, customisable, minimalistic approach to journaling. It was a whole new world to me! Also, given my obsession with ensuring that all my written work looks colourful and aesthetically pleasing, this was a sure-fire way of ensuring simplicity and avoiding the occasional "giving up because it doesn't look perfect" problem that I constantly faced. Bullet Journaling has been one of the only things that I've been able to stick with long-term.

Now, the introductory video on YouTube outlines their process for this, which is great, but the real beauty of Bullet Journaling is that you can customise it to fit your needs. You can be as simple or as decorative with this as you like, but I suggest keeping it fairly plain, simply because that keeps it easy to do and easy to stick with.

JULY 2018

1. SMOOTHIE SUNDAY!
2. BREAKFAST MEETING! / UT HEALTH CENTRE
3. MEETING W/ JIM / CALL W/ KARI
4. HAPPY B'DAY AMERICA! / FIREWORKS!
5.
6.
7.
8.
9.
10.
11.
12.
13.
14.
15.
16.
17.
18. IMPACT RETREAT
19. IMPACT RETREAT
20. IMPACT RETREAT
21.
22.
23.
24.
25.
26.
27.
28.
29.
30.
31.

JULY 2018

☐ FILE FOR LLC
☐ CREATE INFOGRAPHICS
☐ TRAVEL
☐ FINISH READING HAPPY CITY
☐

This brings me to one of my pet peeves related to Bullet Journaling. Every so often, an article or video on Bullet Journaling will start circling across social media and it'll show all kinds of planner spreads that are beautiful and very creative, but they don't even have bullets!!! That is NOT Bullet Journaling. It's just...journaling. So please, don't be THAT person.

Chapter 3

BECOMING A GREAT COMMUNICATOR

America's #1 Fear

Public speaking is often cited as the biggest fear people have. Yes, that's right. There are studies that show people are more afraid of speaking in front of a crowd than they are of dying painful deaths! That sounds really weird to me because I LOVE speaking in front of crowds. I'm the person who is in their flow when I'm sharing a message that I'm passionate about with other people. Sometimes that's in front of a live audience and sometimes it's in front of a camera, but I love it all!

But the relevant question is, do *you*? And honestly, whether you like and enjoy public speaking the way I do or not, you have to acknowledge its importance. If you can communicate effectively with people and share powerful messages, you can succeed in just about anything. Often, the greatest leaders aren't those with the greatest ideas, they're the ones who can communicate their good ideas to the world.

How to Become a Great Speaker

There are loads of tools available to help you in your quest for becoming a great speaker, including workshops, videos, books etc. and they're all great tools. But nothing beats actually practising in front of a live audience. To this effect, I highly recommend taking a speech class (or many), joining a speech and/or debate club, joining Toastmasters International, and finally, hiring someone like me to coach you.

I can assure you that, even though some people who have known me for a very long time would say that I'm a natural-born speaker, there's no way that I would be a GREAT speaker if it weren't for having done all of the things I just listed. If it weren't for my ability to seek out these resources and practice my speaking skills, I wouldn't have the opportunities that I've been blessed to receive, like speaking at events all over the world, speaking at conferences, coaching other individuals who want to better their skills, or even giving a TEDx talk!

So, obviously, taking a speech class or joining a speech and debate club are your on-campus options for improving your speaking skills, but you can also seek out additional involvement opportunities. For example, Model United Nations is a great way to combine your research and speaking skills along with being on a debate team or even presenting your own research at conferences. Some universities have Toastmasters clubs on their campuses, but I would recommend finding a club that isn't just college students. This will greatly help with feedback and improving your skills because those members will most likely all be at different stages in their speaking journeys.

Personally, I attended a workshop before I started university and that really gave me a newfound sense of confidence in my skills. This was before I thought that I might be a good speaker; I just wanted to try something new. I invited my friends to join me, but none of them had the courage to say yes, so my dear mum accompanied me! And we had a blast. In fact, that was the moment when someone told me for the first time that I need to pursue speaking as a way of life and source of income. So, with this newfound belief and encouragement, I started pursuing opportunities for myself to accomplish this goal while at university.

While I may have more experience with speaking than most people my age, I'm still on a journey to become a great speaker. When I watch my favourite speakers give talks, I'm constantly motivated to improve and get to their level. But during my time as an aspiring professional speaker and now *being* a professional speaker, I have learnt a thing or two. So, I'll be covering a few "Dos and Don'ts" that I believe are crucial to your speaking journey during your collegiate experience.

But, before I start, I want to mention two books that I would highly recommend to anyone and everyone who wants to become a better speaker: *The Book on Public Speaking* by Topher Morrison, the person I consider to be speaking #GOALS and *Talk Like TED* which really helped me organise my TEDx Talk well. The former is a very comprehensive guide to speaking and becoming a professional speaker, while the latter is focused on the crux of your presentation. Both are highly valuable and have positively impacted my speaking abilities.

Now on to MY tips and tricks...

Power Poses

Power posing is one of my favourite little tricks when it comes to preparing to get on stage. A great TED talk about this concept is titled "Your body language may shape who you are" by social psychologist, Amy Cuddy. While some of the findings in the talk have been controversial, I swear by the Super(wo)man pose.

 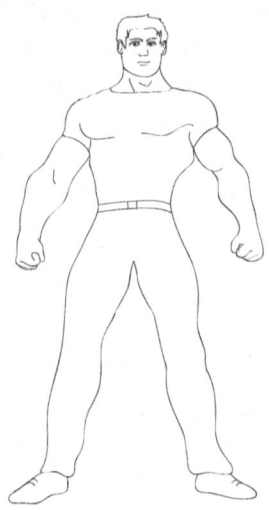

Smile!

In conjunction with power posing is smiling! A research study conducted at the University of Kansas found that smiling helps reduce the body's response to stress and lowers your heart rate in tense situations. Even if you're like me and you enjoy speaking, your physiological state before you go up and give a talk is almost always going to be a little tense or stressed. Therefore, power posing with a big smile on your face may seem silly at first, but it does the trick, I promise!

What to Wear

Dress well, but dress comfortably well. By that I mean, don't wear sweatpants or leggings because you shouldn't be wearing them anywhere other than the gym or your bed because they're NOT real pants, but I digress. My "go to" outfit choice is business casual, always. But, depending on the situation, you may want to go with business professional, casual or a costume, but whatever you choose, make sure that your outfit matches the tone and subject you're speaking about, is aligned with the expectations of the people you're addressing, and above all, helps you feel confident about yourself and your appearance.

For example, when I gave my TEDx talk, I wore one of my favourite dresses and a pair of comfortable heels. With a TEDx talk, there aren't really many rules for what you should wear, but you have to keep the stage and the logo in mind while picking your outfit. I chose a blue dress because it would stand out without being "too much" and I received several compliments about my outfit. But, one of the first comments on the TEDx Talks YouTube channel (it has since been deleted) was about how my outfit was totally inappropriate for this talk. I don't really understand why, and neither did other people who commented that my outfit was appropriate and gorgeous. The moral of the story is, people will find something wrong regardless of what you wear. So, wear whatever makes you feel most confident.

Eye Contact

Make eye contact with your audience so that you come across as conversational. Especially when you're on stage, it's easy to come across as talking *at* instead of talking *to* and the best talks are those which feel like a personal conversation between a speaker and every member in the audience.

A great way to do this is to pick a person in every corner of the room and look directly at each of them while speaking, instead of just staring into space. This will make everyone in that general direction feel that you are looking at them and you will seem more conversational and personal to your entire audience.

Vocal Techniques

Voice projection and modulation are essential to a great delivery. If you are miked up, you may not need to project your voice the way you would have to if you aren't, but there is still a certain amount of projection that goes into speaking in a way that invites listeners to engage. You need to be loud enough for your audience to hear you clearly, but without actually yelling or shouting. Modulation, though, is a technique that improves your delivery. Modulation is when a speaker changes their tone of voice, their pace, and/or their rhythm during the talk. Maintaining a similar tone, volume, and pace sounds monotonous during a presentation and is certain to bore and disengage your audience, so please, use variety.

Don't Apologise

I've often heard speakers start their talk by apologising for being unprepared. I know, you're not feeling confident, so you're trying to temper your audience's expectations but what you're really doing is reducing your credibility in the eyes of your audience right off the bat, and that is NEVER a good thing. As for apologising for messing up, please don't do that either. The only person who knows your speech is you, so even if you mess up, the audience *probably has no idea*, so don't give it away. You can deliver a presentation with 47,583,627 mess ups and still have it seem flawless in the eyes of your audience!

Ditch the Deck

For some reason, people are really devoted to using PowerPoint or Keynote slideshows during every speech they give, and I really don't understand it. I didn't even use one for my TEDx talk! Unless I absolutely *need* to, I refrain from using slides. First, it detracts from the conversational element of your talk and that conversational feel can so easily make or break your entire presentation! I'm all for simplicity when it comes to creating slides, and if I have to use slides, I usually just use pictures on a white background. This helps to keep me as the focus of the talk rather than the slides, which is what you'll want, and I never put more than a few words on a slide. Oh, and if you do decide to use slides, please memorise them. Don't be the person who needs to see and read their slides because they're so dependent on them for their talk. Your slides should complement your talk, not *be* your talk. No one in the history of presentations has ever talked about that great slideshow they once saw. Your *words* are always the most important element!

Should You Memorise Your Talk?

Memorisation is an interesting technique when it comes to delivering a talk. I have friends who swear by it and will not give a talk that they don't have completely memorised; but personally, I struggle with this. I once memorised an entire speech, and during the final round of a speech contest, I blanked and forgot my speech midway through. I've never memorised a speech word-for-word since. I memorise key phrases and statements that I deem powerful and I recite my speech until I'm extremely familiar with the content; but I don't write out my speeches word-for-word anymore and this has worked very well for me. But, everyone is different, so try several techniques before settling on one. I sometimes use a single notecard with my first and last sentences written out along with three bullets for my three main points. I usually won't look at the notecard, even if I have it in my hand, but it does sometimes help me to feel more confident. So, that's another option as well.

The reason I refer to this as a journey is because there isn't really a destination when it comes to speaking. It's a skill that you need to constantly improve and practice, and if you stop learning and trying to better yourself, you will remain average or might even drop to below average. And who wants that?!

Chapter 4

BECOMING A MORNING PERSON

Growing up, I was convinced that the early bird life was not for me. I had always been one to go to bed quite late. In fact, in high school my average bedtime was 4am. It started when I was much younger and would like to wait for my daddy to get home from work. He worked long hours, so the only time I would see him would be early in the morning or late at night.

My parents encouraged us to be early risers, but it was never a compulsion. Therefore, I did as I pleased and learnt to function despite my lack of sleep. I would pull too many all-nighters during my school days so I could keep up with my academics instead of getting a good night's sleep and waking up early in the morning the next day to study.

I often used those random correlations that you see on your Facebook newsfeed as evidence that I was a smart night owl. In all honesty, I envied people who could wake up early. Despite my best efforts at the time, I was unable to do so, and therefore I stuck to being a night person.

But university changed that for me. I still remember the first morning that I woke up at 5:30am because... I wanted to. It was the winter break after my first semester and I was staying with my mum's friend and her family in Atlanta, Georgia. Before the end of that semester, I had befriended some really amazing people and I was determined to emulate them in many aspects of my life, including my longing for being a morning person. The phrase "the early bird catches the worm" is so overused that it's more of a cliché than anything else; but even then, it doesn't make it any less accurate.

We constantly hear stories of successful people who wake up before the rest of us and are big fans of the early hours. If you haven't already experienced nature's serenity and tranquillity in those hours, you won't understand it until you do. People in my life that I really look up to, including my mentors and friends, are all early risers. They swear by their morning rituals which almost always include a combination of waking up early, exercising, and reading. And I try my best to follow suit.

Waking up early has had so many positive effects on my life that I cannot not be a morning person anymore. I feel so productive and refreshed when I wake up early and start accomplishing my goals before the rest of the world is even awake.

The biggest hurdle to becoming a morning person is your mindset. I know that that was the case for me. I truly believed that I could never become a morning person because I had spent 18 years of my life being a night owl. But guess what? Whether you think you can or can-not do something, that thought will dictate the outcome. When I focused on my deep-seated desire to become a morning person and internalised the belief that I could be one, I was able to change my reality.

How I Did It

If you're not currently a morning person and you've decided to make the switch, here's what I did to make the transition:

I chose to start being a morning person during a break, and not during the semester because I wanted to adjust myself to this new way of life in a more casual setting at first. This made it easier for me personally, but I soon realised that unless I had something to do that morning at the time I woke up, I didn't feel like the effort was worth it. Even now, while I may wake up at 5:30am without even an alarm, I don't feel as accomplished if I don't have any goals to accomplish that morning, so make sure you establish something extremely worthwhile to do when you get up.

An alternative approach that works for some people is to force yourself to wake up by signing up for early morning commitments. If you have a fitness class in the morning or an 8am lecture, you know you can't miss those and that will force you to wake up. I personally don't do well with forceful regulations and hence the first approach works better for me, but if you're someone who does better in this type of situation, that's another option to help you become a morning person.

Finally, having accountability partners that you would not like to disappoint is another big way you can embrace this way of life. If you have a friend who also wants to start becoming a morning person, you can be accountability partners for one another and hold each other accountable to waking up at a certain time. Another technique would be to ask your mentor to hold you accountable, especially if they, too, are early risers.

It's true that not every single successful person is an early riser, but a good majority of the types of people I would like to be around are. From business leaders to political leaders, there are so many inspiring people who wake up well before the rest of the world, and science says that that is how they are able to succeed where most people do not.

Chapter 5

TAKING CARE OF YOUR SOUL

This entire chapter can be summed up by the quote "Find God but leave the dogma", from Macklemore's song "Growing Up" but if you would like to read a story of transformation, please continue.

Religion is something most people grow up with or around. Even though 22.8 percent of America's population identifies as unaffiliated, most people today are surrounded by one world religion or another. I grew up in an Indian household with lots of cultural aspects of Hinduism affecting my day-to-day life. But, I went to a Christian school for 12 years and let me tell you, I know the Lord's Prayer and other Christian hymns way better than I know any Hindu hymns. Some of that might have to do with the fact that English is my first language and no Hindu hymns are in English. But I also grew up with friends who were Muslim, Zoroastrian, Jain etc. and I never looked at any of them as being wrong.

Rebel Juhi

For a brief period of time, during my "rebel" years, I thought it was so stupid for anyone to believe in religion and/or God and I constantly looked down on people who were religious or spiritual. This was mostly because I resented my parents for forcing me into Hinduism when I didn't believe in any of its tenets at the time, and the internet told me it was cool to be atheist. It was also because I realised there was no concrete evidence of God existing. And finally, my rebel kid phase had me rebelling against all forms of structure and, for better or worse, God and religion fell under this category.

My rebellion against religion did not, however, mean I didn't enjoy the communal and festive aspects of it. I was still pleading with my parents to bring Lord Ganesha to our house in 2013 while I was still forcing my friends to come to a Christmas Eve service at a big church and I was still always looking for an excuse to dress up in traditional Indian wear.

So, until I came to university, I happily subscribed to atheism because that made the most sense to me with the knowledge I had at the time. But, soon after coming to college, I realised that I didn't actually "know" either way. After being introduced to the concept of agnosticism in my first semester of university, I quickly decided that this would be my new truth. Since I didn't have proof either way and almost no interest in pursuing any further truth, I was going to be agnostic.

New Friends

Even though I was firm in my non-pursuit, I was still a tiny bit curious. But it wasn't until my second semester that I befriended someone who was *very* religious. My friend was a Protestant Christian and very evangelical, at that. While I respected his beliefs, I couldn't help but wonder how he knew what he said he knew. How could he know for sure that God existed, or that Christianity was the best way to pursue a relationship with this God? This was also around the time that I befriended another individual who was Catholic. And while my two friends believed in the same ideas, they disagreed over what the right way was to pursue their beliefs. Each believed their own way to be the right way, and this puzzled me even further because both of these people were so closed off to the notion that the other could be right!

After some time went by, though, I decided that I wanted to learn more about religion and God, and maybe even find a new truth for myself. Hence, I enrolled in the World Religions course offered by my university. This was a very scary moment for me because I knew that at the end of this class, I could possibly change my entire philosophy on religion and God and I was afraid to find out what that would mean for my identity. Dismissing all this fear, I decided I would go through it even if it led to an existential crisis.

The First Big Influence

My World Religions class turned out to be one of the most interesting and educational classes I have taken at university. My professor was a darling, and she and I became very close. So much so, that we kept in touch even after the class was well over. It was so incredible to see her put aside her personal beliefs about religion and deliver a very unbiased educational experience about something so personal for most people. The class taught me about so many religions that I had not even heard of, all the while teaching me more about the ones

I was familiar with. I was even able to visit some interesting "religious" places for class visitations.

This class was a great step in becoming more aware of all the different religions that exist in the world and in understanding why people are so easily offended when someone criticises their religious beliefs. My primary takeaway was that it is very important to understand what one holds sacred.

The Next Big Influence

By the end of the semester, I had holiday plans in Dubai with some of my family and friends. On this trip, a friend who was well aware of my philosophy and my spiritual journey gifted me a book. This book was *Code Name God* by Mani Bhaumik. Mani Bhaumik is the scientist who discovered the practical use of laser technology which resulted in the LASIK eye surgery technology. The book is an incredible saga of his journey with spirituality and his search for God, and he does such a great job at creating connections between spirituality and science. He is well-versed in Quantum Physics, which is a discipline I've always been rather interested in and it was eye-opening to learn about how many similarities there are between the principles of quantum mechanics and the idea of God.

Someone close to me who knew I was trying to make sense of the idea of God and my beliefs and wanted to know what was truly out there suggested that I pray to God and ask God to show me that God exists. Now, this was something that required a true leap of faith and I was not sure if I wanted to try this. After days of contemplation, I figured it was worth a try and so I gave it a shot. Days went by and I didn't notice or feel anything different. Days turned into weeks and I still didn't notice anything different.

Then one day, as I was talking to myself (something I do way more often than I would like to admit), I felt like someone or something was listening. Not in a scary or creepy way, but in a loving way. As if this entity cared and wanted me to know that it was there for me. I was very uncomfortable at first and thought my head was just making something up. I even checked to see if I was actually awake! After confirming that I was, in fact, awake, I knew something was different. I still hadn't figured what it was, but I knew that something had changed.

And ever since, things have just been different. I now address all my prayers of gratitude to God and try my best to give up my worries to God. I understand and appreciate science and truly believe that science and God are not mutually exclusive. In fact, they are more connected than anything.

I am telling you my personal journey with religion and spirituality, not because I want you to do as I did, but because I believe that if you resonate with something, you should pursue it, even if you're unfamiliar with it. And if you do not resonate with something, there is nothing wrong with exploring new things and challenging your truth. And finally, if you do not resonate with anything, that's also all right. I still don't think I resonate with any organised religion and I know people much older than I am who I respect and admire who also don't resonate with any organised religion. And, my idea of God is not consistent with the traditional idea of any major world religion. I don't believe in ascribing any human qualities to God and instead believe in a loving source of energy and creation. My big message is not to follow something just because others around you are doing so. Your relationship with God is just that– yours. Don't allow other people to dictate it. That will never bring you true love or peace and that defeats the purpose altogether.

I personally believe that it's important for you to have something to believe in and find relief in, even when everything around you is going wrong, but this cannot be forced. You are on your own journey, and when the timing is right, you will find what you need.

While you should not let other people dictate how you pursue religion or God, you can learn from those who have been in your shoes. For me, this spiritual mentor was someone I've never even met, and yet his impact on me was so profound. Your mentor can be someone you know or someone you don't, but it should be someone you admire greatly. Mentors can help you figure out what you should pursue.

My favourite ways of strengthening my relationship with God are writing letters to God and meditating. I don't know of any religion that predicates these as prerequisites to a healthy relationship with God, but this is how I choose to pursue mine. In my letters, I usually start out by thanking God for whatever awesome thing has just happened and expressing my sincere gratitude. I'm not going to detail the benefits of meditation, but I would like to share with you that meditation is not just about sitting cross-legged and thinking about nothingness. It can be rather meditative to doodle, colour, or even practice calligraphy. Any activity that takes your mind off of thinking and worrying and contemplating can be a meditative activity that can bring more mindfulness and peace into your life. In fact, my favourite type of meditation is guided meditation that puts me to sleep!

If you seek something, you will find it. This means that, if you want to believe in God and are actively looking for proof that God exists, you will find it. And if you are looking for proof that God doesn't exist, then that is what you'll find. It's up to you to be open-minded and seek what your heart truly desires. The bottom line is, you should pursue true happiness, peace, and love. Some religions refer to true happiness as joy but the two are interchangeable in my vocabulary. What I mean by peace is peace of mind and contentment. And love is loving yourself, loving those in your life, and loving those you don't even know. A person truly in love with themselves and the world around them can never spread negativity even if they are having a bad day. By aspiring to be this person, you can make the world a happier and a more positive place.

Chapter 6

TAKING CARE OF YOUR MIND & BODY

I'm not the type of person who counts every calorie or micromanages the nutrient content of every bite I consume. I'm also not the type of person who eats pizzas and burgers and drinks aerated beverages all day. I eat relatively healthy for a young person, which by the way can be hard to do in America (just kidding... NOT). I try to balance my meals with veggies and protein and I indulge in some dessert every once in a while. What I strictly do not consume, though, is caffeine. Yes, that's right. A university student who doesn't drink coffee. Yes, we exist! I dislike everything about coffee: the taste, the smell, the cult-like approach of its drinkers, but I digress!

Freshman 15

As a tiny person, I don't generally eat too much. I mean, three meals a day sounds painful to me. I've never been a big eater, and regardless of how much exercise I get, my appetite doesn't change too much. But when I did need to eat, I tried to find food on campus that was relatively healthy. The problem is, I went to university in America! (Okay, I'll stop!) For real, though, campus food is not always healthy and if you grew up with parents who monitored your junk food intake, your cafeteria will be like food heaven to you. My case was really interesting, though, because growing up, my parents let me order pizza all the time because they just wanted to make sure I was eating. As I said, I've never been a big eater, so when I actively wanted to eat something, they never said no. And to a large extent, I really enjoyed simple American food and still do. But watching my peers scarf down pizza slice after slice, and gobble burger after burger was a little too much for me. So, I found myself eating much healthier than I would, say, in India.

After coming to university, I was introduced to the idea of the "Freshman 15." Freshman 15 is this popular notion that students can expect to gain 15 pounds (approx. 7 kilograms) in their first year of college because they either have a newfound sense of freedom that they exercise to eat to their hearts' content or they get homesick and deal with that by overeating or for several other reasons. The focus, though, is food. But you know what? The Freshman 15 may be real, but it will only be a part of *your* reality if you allow it to be.

On-Campus Food

Every campus has food options. According to the Universities department at Sodexo, they service approximately 500 universities in the United States, so there is a very high chance that your institution is one of those. The University of Tampa is one of them. I never had any qualms about the variety or quality of the food and I enjoyed my dining experience. They divide the cafeteria into various sections, so we had a salad bar, a deli, an international food station, an omelette station, pizza and burgers, healthy station, et cetera, so I always had lots of options, and this was just the cafeteria. In addition to this, we had several other food places that were cuisine-specific or more like cafés, and we had a Starbucks! But if you're really trying to eat very healthy, you may want to find a way to opt out of your meal plan. If you have health issues, a note from your doctor will suffice. You can also become a Resident Assistant and that can allow you to opt out of your meal plan. You may want to check with your university first, though.

Another way that you can end up consuming junk food is through snacks. I personally love snacks because I don't like eating too many full meals in a day. And I love chips, but I know that they're not very healthy. So, I eat lots of veggie chips. They are many different brands that you can choose from at your local grocery store. Another option is to find easy snack recipes that you can make in your dorm. There are tons of examples on Instagram and Pinterest, and I've even created a board that you can follow on Pinterest with some recipes that I would recommend!

All in all, don't be too worried about gaining weight when you get to university because there are many different ways you can avoid that. As long as you get enough exercise and eat relatively healthy, you should be just fine!

Taking Care of Your "Self"

During my talk at Ignite Tampa Bay about Active Citizenship, the audience erupted into applause and laughter when I mentioned that "being nice" was an important part of being an active citizen. What I meant by this was that I was kind and open-minded in my dealings with other people, whether separate individuals or groups of people that I had never met before. And this characteristic has taken me a long, long way.

A negative person who is constantly trying to find fault with other people and trying to one-up others is honestly a very sad individual. How do I know this? I know this because, until university, I was that person. I was so insecure and unhappy with myself that I would have to pretend like I was better than everyone else and make other people feel small. The funniest part? I wasn't doing anything worthwhile at the time and so I didn't really have anything to show for my being "better." It was all a sham, and I attracted other people who were just like me. Those friends weren't really good for me, and now when I look back at those times, I realise how most of those people were never really my friends to begin with!

Open-mindedness

When I came to university, I made a mental decision to be open-minded and to give everyone a chance. I wanted to listen more than I talked (I can talk a *lot*) and I wanted to be friends with people from all over the world. This was pretty easy at the University of Tampa and at the University of Oxford because both of them have students from about 140 different countries! As someone who grew up outside of the country I was studying in, there were cultural norms that I observed, but didn't understand. By being respectful and genuinely curious, I was able to get so many of my burning questions answered by people. This included conversations with people about why "the n-word" was so offensive if a non-black person were to say it and the gun problem in the United States. These were very foreign ideas to me and all I wanted was for someone to help me understand.

One of my favourite stories about open-mindedness is that of a friend and their partner. This friend grew up in a household that embraced Islamophobia and they fed into that idea for majority of their life. Of course, at university you meet people from all types of religious and national backgrounds, and soon after coming to university, they befriended someone who was a staunch Muslim from an Arab country. Now, my friend, too, wanted to practice open-mindedness and given that they shared mutual friends with this Muslim individual, they had to be around them occasionally. As the two spent more time together, my friend realised how ridiculous the idea of being prejudiced against someone simply because of their religion was and started truly being open-minded to the Muslim individual. What started as a great friendship soon turned into love and it was incredible to watch that happen because their story shows the power of open-mindedness. This friend would've never met their college sweetheart had it not been for their decision to choose open-mindedness over the unfair narrative that had plagued their childhood and young adulthood.

Open-mindedness is not simply about people, but also about opportunities. Don't be too quick to judge something as lame or not good enough without experiencing it first. I did that with student government in my first semester and assumed that it was lame and didn't create any real change in the university, but after I befriended a past president, I realised how much actually went into it and I became seriously motivated to run for a position. I'm still so grateful for winning and having the opportunity to serve as a senator. I can truly say that it was one of the most rewarding involvement experiences during my time at the University of Tampa. In fact, I even considered running for president, but by then I had found out that I would be studying abroad at the University of Oxford and I was only permitted to choose one.

More than Meets the Eye

Something that you may not think about in terms of diversity is financial backgrounds. All universities have students with extremely wealthy parents and students who are just scraping by. And more often than not, you won't be able to tell who's who. Assuming that all your friends come from a similar financial background as you without confirming it can put you in awkward situations where you may feel less than or someone else might.

There's also a cultural element to this wherein something may be very normal for a middle-class person in your culture but is way out of the norm for someone who may be middle-class in another culture. A personal example from my life was when I would talk about my maid or other house servants with my American friends. As a middle-class household in India, my family was able to afford a full-time maid and 3-4 other task-specific individuals to help around the house like a cook, a washer etc. But this is so out of the norm for even an upper middle class family in America that my friends just couldn't understand. Especially when I would try to explain that my maid was like family to us. I assumed that everyone grew up with help around the house, while my friends assumed that nobody did.

By engaging in open conversation about our life experiences, we realised how different our lives had been to that point and we learnt to not only appreciate our own situations a little more, but we were also able to see the benefit of the others' lifestyles. As someone who didn't know how to make a bed or use a vacuum cleaner until university, I appreciated how independent my friends were growing up. I don't think I'd trade my maid for independence, but I do see the benefit! I miss her so much!!!

Diversity is beautiful. And the ability to appreciate and respect diversity will take you on an incredible learning journey. You can learn about languages, cultures, food, politics, and so much more without even leaving your physical location. I think of it like reading a fiction book that transports you into a different world, but instead, this is just a real conversation with a person who does not look like you or talk like you or think like you. And those are some really special friendships.

There are so many ways to get involved with diversity initiatives at university. You can join different clubs, take classes, talk to people (I know, it can be scary, but *You Got This!*), join dialogue groups and diversity forums, etc. People will accept you for you, if you're willing to accept them for them. You do not have to agree with everything a person stands for to have a real open conversation with them. You just need to share mutual respect for each other and have a shared curiosity about each other.

My closest friends in Tampa are not 20-something year-old Indians, they're people from different parts of the country or the world who are much older than I am and are not aspiring to do what I want to do in my life. And yet, they're all my close friends and I can have incredible conversations with them about anything in the world, and even if we disagree with what the other person has to say, we never disrespect each other. And that, to me, is the real definition of friendship, kindness, and open-mindedness.

Relax, Avoid Burn Out and Be YOU!

As someone with a short attention span, I find it extremely hard to be constantly motivated or focused if I'm not having fun.

College is intense as it is, and my collegiate experience was even more intense because I was trying to graduate early while still being extremely involved and sometimes I found myself burning out. And if you've never experienced burn-out before, I can assure you that it's an awful feeling. You can get burnt-out regardless of how much you enjoy what you're doing, believe in what you're doing, or even are passionate about what you're doing. Burning out is physical as well as mental and can even be spiritual if what you are giving your energy to is not aligned with your values.

Sometimes when I told people that I was feeling burnt-out, their immediate response was that I should slow down and stop doing as much as I was doing. But, while I did recognise the need for a break, I liked the pace of my life. The problem was, living in Tampa it was almost impossible to truly get away from work. So, I started planning weekend getaways, and then in 2017, I made it my New Year's resolution to travel once a month!

As someone who loved travelling, but didn't have a lot of money, even day trips were a luxury; but thanks to the incredible opportunities that God and the people in my life presented to me, I was able to accomplish that goal and travel to many different cities and countries. Whether it was a day trip or a 10-day vacation, I was able to get out of my own head and truly relax and rejuvenate.

Of course, it's much harder to do than it sounds, so here are some easy tips for travelling and taking short breaks:

Road trips are awesome!!! For my first Spring Break ever, I went on a road trip to the Smokey Mountains with some friends and it was awesome! Road trips are often less expensive than air or train travel, especially if you're with other people. Pick a destination that's not more than 5-6 hours away and you can have a fun weekend long trip!

Concerts and music festivals are very popular in college student circles. If that's your kind of fun, find a few people to go with and enjoy a completely different setting. Many of my friends took full advantage of the fact that we were in Florida and made it a point to hit up every major music festival in the state!

Another great way to travel is by attending or participating in conferences. I will go more in detail about this one in Part 3, but by getting your university to help offset the costs and/or earning scholarships to attend conferences, you can get away from your regular life, save money, *and* travel to a different place!

Finally, visiting your friends and family is another way to get a nice break while not spending too much money. If your family can afford to pay for all the travel, then that's awesome, but at the very least you can crash with friends or family and save on hotel costs. That way you can spend more on fun activities and travelling to and from the destination.

A friend of mine, Diane, managed to travel every single weekend of her last semester, simply by attending conferences and visiting friends and family all over the United States!

Even if travelling isn't your idea of a break, find out what is and make sure you include that as part of your monthly plan, because burning out is a real thing that you will want to avoid at all costs. I remember the first time I felt burnt out and it was so awful because I wanted to be productive, but I just didn't have the mental capacity to function. This is also why I started reserving Sundays for my fun days. And occasionally, I'll slip up and get work done on Sundays, but I try my best to just relax and mentally prepare for the upcoming week on that day.

Movies versus Reality

Contrary to popular belief (or more like pop culture belief), college is not just about frat parties and alcohol, and not everyone in college is a big partier! In fact, it is completely fine to not go to parties.

I have friends who party *all the time* and are still getting As and Bs in their classes, and I also have friends who party *all the time* and are almost failing every class. I have friends who *never* party and get As and Bs in their classes and then I also have friends who *never* party and are still almost failing every class. The bottom-line is, whether you choose to go out all the time or not, if you have a plan in place and have your priorities straight, you *will* succeed, and you *will* do well in your academic life. Personally, I don't enjoy the idea of frat parties or clubs because I don't like being surrounded by drunk strangers in small spaces. But if you do enjoy parties where you can meet tons of new people and socialise, then there's nothing wrong with that.

Also, if you're of legal drinking age in the country you are studying in, you can go out to bars or pubs and those are often times more casual and, in my opinion, more fun. When I was in England, the pub culture was so prominent that I often found myself at the pub even if I wasn't drinking (just an FYI, the legal drinking age there is 18). Most people's social lives there were centred around the pub they fancied and would usually be found there after work or lectures.

An important factor to consider when thinking about individuality is the culture you come from. If your culture is a drinking culture or a smoking culture or anything else, you may find yourself in a place that you cannot engage in those behaviours. So, while you should be you, you should also consider the legal and social ramifications of your actions.

Really, You Be You

Another thing I want to touch on is the difference between introverts, extroverts and ambiverts. The best definitions I ever came across for the first two were in my Leadership Studies class where we learnt that introverts are those who get their energy internally and from being around themselves, while extroverts are those who get their energy externally and from being around other people. Then there are ambiverts, myself included, those who get their energy from being around other people but only to a certain extent, after which they need to be reclusive and just be by themselves. I *love* people and I love being around them all day, but at night all I want to do is be by myself, or at the most with a few close friends, and just relax and recuperate and rejuvenate so I can do it all again the next day.

The reason I bring this up is to further highlight the idea that it is A-Okay to be yourself. If you know your limit, it's okay to guard that fiercely, because at the end of the day, you have to prioritise yourself over other people. The only way you can positively impact others to your maximum potential is if you're operating at your maximum potential. So, do whatever you need to do in order to sustain that. BE YOU and the rest will fall into place.

Part 2

IN-FLIGHT NAVIGATION

Chapter 7

ADJUSTING TO YOUR NEW HOME

Moving away from "home", is hard, no matter how much you desire it. It might take some people a few weeks to find a new "home" in their new city, while it may take months, or even years, for others. Either way, you must remember that taking time to adjust is completely okay. Depending on your pre-college financial, social, and geographical circumstances, you may have either been used to sharing a room with someone or you might not be. Most college students spending an average amount of money on their room and board end up sharing rooms with one or more persons.

The Realities of Roommates

A common consequence of living with someone is what I call "roommate fatigue." This is basically when you don't actually have any real issues with your roommate, but the fact that you're always around each other makes you tired of them. It's very likely that at some point in the semester you're going to get tired of living with your roommate and this dissatisfaction can create unnecessary issues that might not even really exist.

For example, your roommate might have always kept his or her book bag on the chair, but one day it might suddenly start being a bother to you. To avoid experiencing this unpleasant condition, it helps to make sure that you have a life outside of your roommate relationship. That is, having other friends you dine with, go out with, and hang out with. Your roommate should not be your only friend, because if something goes wrong with that one relationship, you must be able to get on with your life.

Roommate issues are commonplace, and it doesn't help to ignore them, in my personal experience. The key to a good roommate relationship is the same as the key to any good relationship: *communication*. If something is bothering you, it's better to say something sooner rather than later. If you don't, you're simply going to create tension. That tension will eventually harbour negative emotions towards your roommate and that can lead to big problems.

If things get out of hand and you just can't seem to work things out, don't be afraid to seek outside support. It is your Resident Assistant's job to play mediator in situations like these. If you believe that you just can't live with the person, talk to the housing office and let them know so that they can make alternate arrangements, if that's possible. It's usually easiest to change rooms during the first few weeks when a policy is in place for being able to change your room.

How NOT to Choose a Roommate

While pop culture might drive you to believe you have to be the best of friends with your roommate(s) or else you will become sworn enemies, there is a middle ground. You should not feel pressured to be best friends with your roommates or suitemates. I have personally had more negative roommate relationships than positive, but that doesn't mean that you will. The two lessons I have learnt are: first, DO NOT room with someone from back home; and two, DO get to know any new roommates for a little while before rooming together. Obviously, this calls for story time!

I came to college with my friend from high school. We were super excited about embarking on this new chapter in our lives together. Given that we were both still very young and had overbearing mothers, it was decided that we would room together. All of our friends were very excited for us! Actually, all of our friends but one. This friend was a long-time friend of mine who was already studying in the States at the time, and she was quite sure that it was a bad decision, but I didn't pay attention to her advice, so off we went to college!

Things were *great*! We decorated our room together, made new friends, explored the city – all of that. And then something changed. While I was busy being social and getting involved and loving my new "home", my friend was missing her "home." And I was oblivious to her suffering. That created rifts in our living situation because we were not in sync with our schedules or our social lives anymore. And then it started creating rifts in our friendship because neither one of us was happy that the other was behaving differently from what we expected from one another. Finally, I realised I had to change something or else I would lose my friend forever, so I decided to move out.

I moved in with a girl I knew nothing about, other than that her previous roommate had moved out and into the adjoining dorm room. I didn't know who she was or why she moved out. The first few days with Megan were fine. I was rather unsuspecting. But then the nightmare began. Given my academic and extracurricular involvement, I was hardly ever in the room, but when I was, she would constantly pick fights with me and try to get me in trouble with the Resident Assistant.

One day I'd had enough. I needed answers, so I went to the adjoining dorm room where her previous roommate lived. As soon as we got talking, she told me about all the psychological and emotional abuse she had dealt with while living with Megan. I was horrified! I was accustomed to Megan's door slamming and random rude commentary, but what I didn't know was how long she had been treating other people the same way. Once Megan found out that her previous roommate and I had become friends, she tried to create fights between us! Thankfully, we knew better, and her plans never came to fruition.

At one point, I got an email from the Dean of Residence Life asking me to come and meet her urgently or else I would lose my housing. I was confused and scared, but quite sure that it was another one of Megan's plots. When I went in to talk to the Dean, I was told that Megan felt "threatened" by a mini-poster on my desk that was along the lines of "Nothing can hinder Queen Juhi's path." Now, I was given this poster my someone close to me and I kept it on my desk as motivation along with a few pieces. And once I told the Dean that, even she acknowledged that Megan's claim was a little far-fetched and that I should just deal with her for the next couple of weeks because we were so close to the end of the semester. So, that's what I did.

The next semester I found out that Megan had transferred. That piece of news brought relief to quite a few people. I am sure that she was not that way with everyone in her life, but I most certainly did not have a great relationship with her despite my best efforts. I hope this serves as an example as to why you should not room with someone you're very close to;

and if you do move in with someone else, get to know them a little first.

Universities usually have a window between the first few weeks of a semester that allows you to change your room if you're miserable there. Don't be afraid to exercise this option if you're in a highly uncomfortable situation. And honestly, at any other point in the semester when you feel uncomfortable or unsafe.

Dealing with Homesickness

A good way to cope with homesickness is to make your dorm room more... *you*. You have a lot of freedom in terms of decorating your room, so use that wisely to showcase your unique character. Keeping it positive is key because that will serve as motivation when you really don't feel like being productive. It's helpful to look on Pinterest for ideas. In fact, I've created a Pinterest board for you, to give you some ideas!

One important thing to keep in your room is snacks! We all have those days when we don't want to get out of bed, but our stomach says otherwise. Sometimes, it's too hot or too cold to walk all the way to the dining hall (if you live in the same building as your dining hall, *I envy you*) and you will thank yourself immensely when you can just reach for a snack instead. Even during finals week when you might find yourself losing track of time and crunching numbers and words, munching on snacks can help you stay focused and reduce how much time you waste. I don't suggest loading up on unhealthy foods, but hey, a little chocolate never hurt anyone!

PSA For Commuter Students

Commuter students are students who do not live on university property. The only time I was a commuter student was when I was at Oxford, but I did have lots of friends in Tampa who were commuter students.

Depending on your university, the culture may sway towards on- or off-campus housing for specific years. At Oxford, there were policies that dictated this; but in America, other than some universities making first year on-campus residences mandatory, there is not a specific policy. It's more cultural or unofficial. Upperclassmen tend to live off campus more than underclassmen.

If you are a commuter student, you'll either be driving, cycling, or taking a mode of public transportation to get to and from your residence and the university. Remember, though, that being late to class because it took you too long to find a parking spot or there was too much traffic is not a valid excuse at university. Always aim to get to class early and park somewhere close to where you'll be on the university campus so that you don't have to waste more time walking to get to your destination. If you're taking public transportation, make sure to account for delays and traffic, and plan the route well in advance.

A constant complaint that I heard from my commuter friends was how it was so hard for them to be involved on campus. Most organisations meet in the evenings, so if they were done with classes early, they would have to stick around until the meeting time and often wouldn't want to do that. Without being involved on campus, you won't have the full college experience and you'll regret it later.

One of my friends, Carlos, was a commuter student his whole time at the University of Tampa, but he didn't start getting involved on campus until his senior year. It was great that he realised it, but then he had to try to balance his involvement with his upper-level classes and that wasn't easy to do, either. So, get involved early on so that you can have that proper experience. Then, even if you have to tone down your involvement, which I have had to do, you won't feel too upset because you'll already have experienced a lot of different things!

Chapter 8

MAKING & RETAINING FRIENDS

Keep it Cool

University is a great time to make new friends and meet new people. A word of caution, though! Don't become obsessed with new friends. Nobody appreciates a person who won't leave them alone. I've had this happen to me several times, and I've also seen this happen to other people, and trust me, it gets very annoying very quickly. Clinginess is not attractive, especially when you're new and trying to make friends.

I'm not the best at having close girlfriends, and the two times that I was close to having some, it was really weird. The thing is, I'm sure their intentions were pure, and I'm still good friends with these individuals; but I couldn't consider them my close friends because every time I talk to them for two or three days in a row, they will text me every single day and sometimes even drunk text me! It really does get a little weird.

I appreciate the love, but I'm a low-maintenance friend and I prefer my close friends to be the same way. There are very few people I speak to every single day and that is honestly all I have emotional space for in my life. But, these are girls, and girls are just generally more affectionate in friendships. It's much worse when you are friends with a guy who wants to see you multiple times a day, every single day, despite you not being romantically involved with each other AND gets upset if you hang out with other people.

Being best friends with someone and having those expectations is another thing; being a new friend and being that clingy is not something I would recommend you do. Oh, and the worst thing you can do for yourself is to become overly obsessive with a guy you're romantically interested in! A friend of mine had the biggest crush on a mutual friend of ours and it got to a point where he was legitimately afraid she was stalking him. It was so sad being their mutual friend because I knew she really liked him and just didn't know how to properly express her feelings.

Being creepy is not okay, as a guy or as a girl. #Equality: As a girl, I can honestly say that girls can be just as creepy, if not creepier, than boys; especially because it's so much easier for girls to get away with creepy behaviour. It is NOT cool people, NOT cool.

So even if you're super excited about making new friends, give them their space and don't breathe down their neck; especially if you want to make and retain real friends.

Befriend "Real People"

I don't know if I can stress this enough, but *please* make "real people" friends when you're at university. It's great to have friends who are at your university, but the only way you can ever feel truly at home in the city or town that you're studying in is if you can spend an entire summer there and still have friends to hang out with. And beyond that, it's just so much better for your growth as an individual to be around people who are not just university students.

One of the biggest reasons why I love Tampa and Oxford so much is that I'm involved with the community in those cities and I've made friends there that feel like family. Unless you create something like that for yourself, it's almost impossible to fall in love with a foreign place to such an extent that in just four months you identify it as home over the place you lived in for seventeen years!

I've mentioned this before, but I'll say it again. As a university student, you need to surround yourself with people who are #GOALS in one or multiple areas of your life. If you only have college students in your circle, you're robbing yourself of the opportunity to maximise your potential. That's simply being unfair to yourself.

Another reason to consider making friends outside of the university is in case you end up staying in that place for a longer break and all of your university friends leave to go back home. If that happens, you don't want to be stuck all by yourself and feel miserable and alone.

Especially as an international student, it's critical to find people in the community who want to keep you there, because the way immigration policies are shaping up across the world, you really need to have a strong base of supporters who will stand with you if things are rough. If you are part of a community, it's essential to build relationships with those around you. While they may not always be personal or close friendships, you can also build professional relationships. In a university setting, this includes staff in different offices or departments and professors. They're professionals, too!

Benefits of "Real People" Friends at Your University

Every university employs several staff members who are responsible for fundraising, student life, housing, orientation activities, etc. These are individuals with the most know-how of how that aspect of the university works and they're the best people to help with something you may need from that office. Every university also has several departments and colleges, and these have staff members who can help you if need be. All of these individuals are also aware of on-campus job opportunities and if you show that you're eager to work with them, they'll keep you in mind first if such an opportunity arises.

All of my on-campus jobs were a result of the professional relationships I forged with staff members and faculty. In fact, some of the positions didn't even exist until I was hired for the job and we basically created the job description as we went along. It was awesome! They were all in completely different offices and my duties were very different, too, but given that they all knew about my speaking abilities, all of them focused on that in some way or another.

For one of those jobs I was dealing with current students. For another job I was dealing with alumni. For one more it was a combination of both. The bottom line is, though, that I would've never been offered those opportunities had it not been for the professional friendships I had with the decision makers at those offices. They knew me and liked me, and one thing to remember is: people *really* like to work with people that they like and trust. In fact, even though I wasn't in the College of Business, I was able to take an entrepreneurship class and even do an independent study with a faculty member in that department.

Even during my time at Oxford, I developed many great relationships with individuals all across the university, and that helped me immensely with organising the Hult Prize competition when I was studying there. Another instance was when I was looking desperately for a book that was unavailable except for an exclusive copy and a librarian at one of the libraries in Oxford permitted me to use that copy while writing an important paper.

Building meaningful relationships like these is important, and while it can seem intimidating or hard to build a friendship with someone who works for the university, saying it's beneficial is a gross understatement.

Chapter 9

STAYING SAFE

The intention of this chapter is to not scare but to make you more aware of what you will be dealing with and surrounded by during your time at university.

See Something, Say Something

A phrase that has stuck with me since my first week of university is "See something, say something!" It's a motto that my university really tries to impress upon its students when it comes to safety concerns. The idea is very simple. If you see something unusual or suspicious, you should say something to someone and report it. Even if it turns out to be nothing, it's better to be proactive than reactive when it comes to safety. Your alertness and concern will not only protect you, but also those around you.

Sexual Safety

Since the start of the #MeToo movement, sexual assault has become more of an active conversation than it has ever been. But the reason it became as wildly popular as it did was because of the momentum it had gained over the years. I would highly recommend that you watch the documentary *The Hunting Ground* on Netflix or any other streaming service. While things are not always as scary as the documentary portrays, it is well known that most institutions try to bury cases of sexual assault for the sake of their brand or image. Additionally, victims don't always feel comfortable coming forward to report such incidents and that adds to the number of unreported cases. While sexual assault is commonly thought of as a man doing harm to a woman, there are several cases in which a woman may come to take advantage of a man, and if this is ever a situation you find yourself in as a man, *please* remember that it does not make you any less of a man to report it and seek the help you require. Any human being violating another is a crime and should be treated as such, regardless of what the popular narrative may be.

In the United States, under Title IX of the Education Amendments of 1972, university officials are required to institute a procedure to properly handle complaints regarding sexual harassment, sexual assault, sexual violence, et cetera, and will lose federal funding if they don't comply. The law has several nuances to it that I won't go into detail about, but you can find more information about it online.

I was part of the OneStudent Campaign at the University of Tampa, which is an organisation and campaign initiative started by two incredible women, Kelly Addington and Becca Tieder. They strongly believe that one sexual assault is one too many and that even one student can make a difference! I had the pleasure of working on a short film for their campaign a couple of years ago, which can be found on the "OneStudentOrg" YouTube channel. These women are so innovative and brilliant in their approach to educating students about sexual assault and consent. They even created these card decks called Sexversations to encourage people to talk about this important topic. In fact, they were the ones to tell me about the documentary, and watching it, I was stunned. I had some context to the content of the film, but nothing could have prepared me for the horror stories depicted in it. Even as I type this out, I have goosebumps from just thinking about that film.

Alcohol Safety

I talked a little bit about this earlier, but in a lot of cultures, drinking is not encouraged in the family setting. Especially if there are strict laws prohibiting underage drinking in the country. The United States happens to be one of these countries, so sometimes you'll find yourself around students who have a newfound sense of freedom and no clue as to how they should manage it. So, they go berserk.

If you're going to drink during your time at university, it's important to consider a few things. First, the law! This is especially true in the United States where some students will get fake drivers' licenses to abet their drinking habits. It's very important to understand that if you do get caught, you can mess up your legal record for the rest of your life, because, depending on the situation, you may get charged for a misdemeanour or even a felony. Especially if you are an international student because getting into legal troubles can have severe consequences on your legal status in the country. In the United Kingdom, most people that study at university are of legal drinking age because it's only 18 there; but even so, you must present your identification everywhere you go.

Legal issues aside, you must also pay attention to a few other things to ensure your safety and wellbeing.

The first: *know your limit*! If you're someone who feels tipsy after just a couple drinks, pace yourself! There's no reason to do shot after shot if you know that you won't be able to handle it. The infographic below is a simple guide to what 1 drink of different types of alcohol looks like in a red solo cup and in "appropriate" glasses–

1 pint of beer   =   1 glass of wine   =   1 shot of liquor

Alcohol Poisoning

It's important to know your limit and control your intake because nearly 32 million adults in the United States over the age of 18 were found to be binge drinkers by the National Institute on Alcohol Abuse and Alcoholism. This study revealed that a large number of people in the United States drink at very high levels and it emphasised the dangers associated with such 'extreme' binge drinking, because it's been observed that from the nearly 90,000 people who die from alcohol each year, more than half die from injuries and overdoses associated with high blood alcohol levels.

This pattern isn't just observed in the United States. According to a World Health Organisation report, the per capita consumption of alcoholic beverages globally, equals 6.13 litres of alcohol for every person aged 15 years or older, although there are large variations based on geographical location. The highest levels of alcohol consumption were found to be in more economically developed countries, mostly the Northern Hemisphere, and in some other countries like Argentina, Australia, and New Zealand. The lowest levels of alcohol consumption were found to be in parts of North Africa and sub-Saharan Africa, the Eastern Mediterranean region, southern Asia, and the Indian Ocean. A World Health Organisation Survey on Alcohol and Health found that the five-year trend of drinking among 18–25-year-olds indicated that, out of 82 responding countries, 80 percent showed an increase.

The reason I'm giving you all these statistics is so that you can avoid becoming exactly that—a statistic. You do not want to be just another number that someone cites when talking about alcoholism and binge drinking. Especially not at such a young age! Alcoholism is a real illness and can instantly take over your life, and severe alcohol poisoning can literally take your life.

Other Illegal Substances

You can't talk about alcohol and not talk about illegal drugs when examining safety, so here we go...

Depending on the university you're at, there may be certain types of drugs that are more prevalent than others. Some universities have a high usage of "study drugs," while some have a high usage of "recreational drugs." Again, the legal side of things is an important consideration. For example, smoking marijuana in the state of Colorado in the U.S. is legal, whereas smoking marijuana in the state of Texas is not. Besides that, given that it is still declared illegal in the United States at the federal level, you can still get into legal jeopardy anywhere. In fact, the University of Colorado in Boulder's official Code of Conduct states that they are very strict about the consumption of marijuana on campus. Even though the state of Colorado has passed a constitutional amendment to legalise the consumption of marijuana, there is a federal law prohibiting its possession and consumption, and under the Drug Free Schools Act the university has to prohibit marijuana as well.

Study drugs are fairly common, and according to the Addiction Centre, university students are two times more likely to misuse Adderall than their peers who aren't in college. If you're unfamiliar, Adderall is a prescription drug used in the treatment of Attention Deficit Hyperactivity Disorder (ADHD). The most common usage is for increasing productivity or focus, pulling all-nighters, suppressing appetite or even to simulate feelings of euphoria and confidence. Again, depending on the university you're at, more hard-core drugs like cocaine could be more common and may still be considered study drugs because of the increased focus and simulation it provides. However, this is highly illegal and extremely dangerous for your mental and physical health, and getting caught with possession or usage of cocaine can have much more dire consequences than alcohol.

These drugs are highly addictive and, while university can sometimes be a stressful or anxiety driven environment, the cons of drug use will never outweigh whatever benefit you may think you're receiving.

The One Nobody Talks About

Now that we've talked about some very obvious stuff, I want to talk to you about the most commonly used and yet, not-talked-about-enough drug: *caffeine*! I dream of a world where people will wake up every single morning with a smile on their faces and purpose in their hearts and *no desire for coffee*. Why? Regular consumption of caffeine in the form of coffee or energy drinks alters your brain's chemical makeup leading to fatigue, headaches, and nausea if you try to quit.

Even though scientists established caffeine's addictive nature back in 1994, it wasn't until 2013 that the Diagnostic and Statistical Manual of Mental Disorders (DSM) finally recognised caffeine withdrawal as a mental disorder. Yes, this is a real addiction, but our society has deemed it to be more socially acceptable to partake in it than not to. As someone who has never been a coffee drinker (although, I did have an energy drink phase in the past), I just don't understand it. To me, it's as though coffee addicts are members of a cult. They're so obsessive, and frankly, it's just scary.

Caffeine addiction is real, and unfortunately, this is one addiction that nobody talks about. And at university, you'll find free coffee everywhere. There's even a running joke about how "free coffee" is every university student's favourite two words combined, and that if you advertise anything with that you'll get a large showing. Trust me, you can be a perfectly great student without consuming gallons of coffee or multiple six-packs of energy drinks. *You Got This!*

Eating Disorders

The last type of safety issue I want to address is eating disorders. In the university environment, this is more common than you might imagine. Research shows that full-blown eating disorders typically begin between 18 and 21 years of age and this also happens to be the dominant age group for university students. The increased social pressure and overall stress can lead to a whole array of disorders, including but not limited to, binge eating, anorexia, and bulimia. As we talked before in the previous section, students tend to eat more junk food after being out their parents' watchful eyes and may either eat too much or not enough. According to the National Eating Disorders Association, 35 percent of "normal" dieters progress to pathological dieting. And research has also found that of those individuals, 20–25 percent progress to partial- or full-syndrome eating disorders. Eating disorders are actually the mental illness with the highest mortality rate, so this makes early detection, intervention, and treatment critical to recovery.

Chapter 10

ADDRESSING SAFETY ISSUES

Universities want you to succeed. They really do. The amount of resources available for you is honestly underrated. If you need help for your academic needs, there's a resource available. If you need help for your physical health, there's a resource available. If you need help for your psychological health, there's a resource available. You get the point.

The previous chapter outlined some safety concerns and this chapter will now focus on addressing them and making you aware of the resources that exist to help counter those problems.

Emergency Situations

If you find yourself needing immediate help in the face of an emergency, you should call your Campus Safety or University Police hotline as well as 911. If it's serious enough, the former will call the latter on your behalf anyway, but it doesn't hurt to go ahead and call both to assure your personal safety as well as the safety of whoever is with you. Sometimes universities have protocols in place and will make you aware of these during Orientation Week, but if you're not provided with any specific instructions, you can follow the procedures I just mentioned. Sometimes, your university may even create hotlines for specific situations, so if you find yourself in one of those, the relevant hotline number will be your most helpful call.

Title IX and Sexual Misconduct

In the case of any type of sexual misconduct, there are various resources at your disposal. You can contact your Campus Safety or University Police officers and report incidents to them (you may even have a Victim Advocacy practitioner you can contact), and you can also talk to any faculty or staff member you trust and feel close to. But, please remember that under Title IX, they are obligated to report the incident and get you help. This may not seem like a great thing in the moment, but you deserve justice and care, and that will help you get both. There are specific individuals who are Title IX coordinators who will help you deal with the matter in its entirety.

Healthcare Options

The United States of America is notorious for its expensive health care system, but universities either have health centres on campus or great partnerships with local hospitals making healthcare available to students for free or at very low cost. This includes health services like treatments, prescriptions, physical check-ups, mental health counselling and check-ups,

STD testing, et cetera, all made available to students under their health insurance.

However, emergency medical costs are relatively high in America and that is something you should be aware of. While people seem to constantly call ambulances in the movies and TV shows, the average American most certainly does not. It could cost you close to a thousand dollars to call an emergency ambulance! So, be aware of your university's specific policies for emergency situations and remember to have a plan, just in case.

Students of Concern

The Students of Concern programme at my university was incredible. The essence of it was that if you know of someone who is not in the best of mental health and is engaging in self-destructive or harmful behaviour, you can report them anonymously and they will be called in for a chat with a specialist.

This has helped my friends who have personally dealt with eating disorders and self-harm. They said that if it weren't for such a programme, they would've spiralled down some really dark rabbit holes and are so grateful that someone reported them. The idea behind such a programme is that some people who need help may not be in a stable enough state to seek it themselves. So, someone close to them who is worried about them, can report them anonymously and protect their own identity and their relationship with the person that they're close to. If you are close to someone suffering from an eating disorder, anxiety, depression, alcoholism, addiction, et cetera, you can report them through this programme and they will not be told who reported them.

Counselling Services

As someone who suffers from Seasonal Affective Disorder (SAD), I have personally benefitted from the free counselling services at my university. Seasonal Affective Disorder is a form of depression that people experience at a particular time of year or during a particular season. While most people experience a happier mood when it is sunny outside or less energy when it's gloomy, those of us with SAD experience major depression and its symptoms.

It can be hard to imagine suffering from acute SAD in the Sunshine State of America, but I can assure you that it is possible and even common. The winter months, all over the world, are hard for someone like me and I have come to accept that as a part of my life. Even having grown up in Bombay, India and then lived in Tampa, Florida, I had experienced SAD in the past and I knew that living in Oxford would be worse. But I didn't realise how bad it would get for me until I actually got there. As a high-functioning individual, it's overly upsetting for me when I'm unable to accomplish my goals, but I had to learn to be loving and kind towards myself even on days when I just couldn't get out of bed.

A big part of managing the disorder was being proactive. I started taking Vitamin D pills and going to yoga; and my incredible housing manager, Adam, even arranged for me to have full spectrum SAD lights in my room. Back in Tampa, one other way that helped me manage the disorder was talking to a counsellor.

Nutrition Counselling

Another free resource at my university was Nutrition specialists. This was an awesome resource for me in my last semester there because I wanted to learn more about how I could ensure that I was fulfilling my nutritional requirements on a budget. My counsellor sat down with me, asked me what my goals were, and helped me stay focused on learning easy, simple recipes that were both nutritious and delicious! If your university offers this service, I would HIGHLY recommend utilising it!

Breaking Rules

If you ever want to bend or break any rules, you have to first know the rules.

Every institution has a handbook of your rights and responsibilities as a student, and this is the first place that you should look to if you ever find yourself in a sticky situation, especially when it comes to drugs and alcohol, violence etc. At my university we had a zero-tolerance policy for drugs, but a 3-time warning for alcohol. This meant that, if you were caught with alcohol, you would have two more chances until you were in deep trouble. In the case of drugs, though, you would be kicked off campus immediately if you were an on-campus resident, and you faced the possible threat of expulsion.

It's very important to know if your university has any zero-tolerance policies, and if they do, what they are. You always have to know what you can get away with, especially if you're the type of person who is prone to getting into trouble. You should not be in a situation where you face the possibility of being kicked off campus, put on probation, or expelled, because that will hamper your future at the institution and negatively impact your overall experience at the university. It may even affect your access to registering for classes, extracurricular opportunities, awards and scholarships, events, et cetera.

I was a member of the Student Conduct board at the University of Tampa, and this was basically a small student committee that sat in on disciplinary hearings and made recommendations for what action should be taken to reprimand students who were in trouble for breaking university policies. This gave me a great inside view into how the process works, and while it may sometimes seem unfair if you are the person being punished, I can assure you that nobody intentionally wants to be harsh. There is a policy in place to keep unnecessary troublemakers in check and that is present in every organisation you will ever be a part of.

Chapter 11

ACADEMIC SUCCESS

Choosing a Major

Picking a major can be hard, but it's the first step to being a successful student. Unless you major in something you love, you won't fully enjoy the incredible academic experience your university has to offer. I entered university as a Psychology major and before the end of my first term, I knew I needed to change my major, so I did! I majored in Political Science, and I can tell you that was the perfect major for me. It was the only discipline that got me all hyped and excited about going to class *every single day*. I just loved learning about how the world used to work, how it currently works, and how we can make it work better! In my worldview, there's nothing more interesting than that.

Making a Plan

Picking a major is one thing but planning out your classes for your time at university is another, and it's a *big one*. I created my 3-year plan in my first semester of college and that really helped me stay on track with my graduation goals of graduating with my major and a minor or two with room to study abroad with an Honors distinction, all in 3 years' time. By starting it early on, you can maximise its benefits and plan your whole academic experience well in advance.

Of course, it's important to note that not everything will work out exactly the way you plan it, but having a plan makes you much more likely to accomplish the goal, so I highly recommend doing it. Whether you want to take three years or six years to complete your degree, plan that out and you'll know which requirements you need to fulfil in order to graduate in your desired time frame.

It's hard for me to give you specific information about this because every university has different criteria that you need to fulfil, but a general rule of thumb for a liberal arts university is that there are general requirements you need to fulfil in order to graduate, such as natural science classes, social science classes, mathematics, et cetera, along with specific requirements for your major(s) and minor(s).

Attending Class

By majoring in what you like, you'll be highly motivated to attend class and this leads to several other benefits! First, if attendance is mandatory, you'll have a great attendance score. That can come in handy if you're on the border between two grades. It will also help you build a strong relationship with your professor, which you can leverage for recommendation letters, deadline extensions, rounding up grades, et cetera.

I was once able to give an exam a month later than the rest of my class because I just didn't have the time to study properly and my professor was so understanding about the situation! But, if other students asked for even slight extensions, my professor would probably not say yes to them.

Of course, this doesn't *always* work. I once got scored a 0 for submitting a paper 10 minutes late and I was obviously very unhappy about this. This particular professor was by far my least favourite professor anyway and it seemed like he had an issue with me; yet, I always tried to make peace. So much so that he once mentioned what his favourite cookies were, and in a bid to score some brownie points with him, I even brought him those cookies and he was *still* not very nice to me! I never had to take another class with him again, so it all worked out in the end. And, while I didn't enjoy him very much, I loved the content of the class and it has played a major role in my academic career.

Foundational Courses

I love liberal arts and I love that every student has to take classes in various disciplines, because I believe that is the key to becoming a well-educated individual. However, not every university has a mandatory requirement for each of these following classes and I believe that everyone, regardless of their major, should try these classes out.

The first one is public speaking. Yes, you can study speech and rhetoric in the classroom, and while not everything your professor tells you will be aligned with what a professional speech coach will tell you, there is a lot of value that can be gained from taking a speech class. In fact, take as many as you like, but definitely take at least one. By taking a speech class, you'll have many chances for performance and improvement and that is so important for each one of us. And learning the theory behind some rhetoric and communication content will give you a deeper understanding of the principles you are advised to follow.

The next class is an introductory world affairs or political science class. I know that this may come across as biased given that I'm a Political Science major, and it probably is, but how is it not important to study about the world? My philosophy in life is that it's important to gain a deeper understanding of a system before you can disrupt it for positive change and we all know that the world we live in is a crazy place. But how can we change that if we don't understand it?

The final class is world religions. As someone who doesn't consider herself religious, I can assure you that this class helped open my mind profoundly. This class taught me the importance of religion in some people's lives and how much impact it can have. Learning about people's religions is important for cross-cultural communication and engagement, and if you're opposed to organised religion, this class will teach you exactly why other people are so in favour of it.

Of course, there are many other classes that I took and loved, and I'm always happy to recommend more; but at the very least, try to take these three because they will all have a profound impact on your life.

How to Take Notes

Attending class is great, but taking good notes is even better! And when you do take notes, writing them out has been found to be more beneficial than typing them on your laptop. A study conducted by social scientists Pam A. Mueller and Daniel M. Oppenheimer found that students who took notes on laptops performed worse on conceptual questions than students who took notes longhand because the use of laptops results in shallower processing of the information. This study is widely cited by professors and teachers all over the world and may result in your professor having strong opinions about the use of technology in the classroom, so beware!

After you take notes in class, it's helpful to go back and revisit those notes, looking at the textbook and/or slideshow that the professor may have provided to create even more comprehensive notes and outlines. These are very beneficial during exam time and you can even show them to your professor beforehand to get additional feedback on the content!

Where to Sit

My preference is to always sit in the front row because I have a terrible attention span and get distracted very easily. By sitting in front, I'm always engaged with the material and visible to the professor. Not only will this help them remember you, but it will also help you stay focused and less distracted because it's much harder to get away with using your phone or laptop inappropriately if you're sitting right under the professor's nose. Sitting up front also helps you to engage with the material better. You're more prone to reading the material, asking questions, and even answering questions.

How to Study

Some classes may have study guides available that can be purchased. I personally prefer to make my own notes while studying instead of relying on study guides, because I learn best by writing things down. I kind of explained my studying process but to be more specific, I will rewrite my notes from class and use any terms sheet or review sheet that the professor may provide and make more verbose notes that are clear to understand and easy to read. Then, I'll familiarise myself with the content and make note of anything that I don't recall or understand and ask the professor any questions I still have.

Eating in Class

When I was in school, eating in class was highly discouraged, so it was always thrilling to get away with munching on snacks while the teacher was looking away. Unfortunately, I brought this habit to university and soon realised that not every professor was cool with students eating during the lecture. In my experience, professors that taught during lunch time (around 12pm) were the most lenient when it came to students eating in class; and as common courtesy, snacks were preferred to full meals. If you need to eat, though, it's always best to check with the professor beforehand instead of getting them upset with you.

Don't Overlook Office Hours

Another way to gain favour with professors is going to office hours! Essentially, "office hours" is a certain time during the week that professors set aside for students to come in and ask questions, discuss problems, or get help with something. By being a regular at their office hours, you have the opportunity of engaging one-on-one with your professor. This helps to build that strong professional relationship as well.

Plagiarism

Plagiarism is taken very seriously at university. If you studied the International Baccalaureate Diploma Programme for 11th and 12th grade like I did, you may already be familiar with the Turnitin® software. It is a plagiarism-checking software programme that most universities employ to ensure that all your submissions are truly yours and not copied from somewhere on the internet. I knew it was taken seriously, but I did not know the extent until a friend of mine got in trouble and was failed from the class and reported to the conduct office. While he was able to retain his position at the university, it was a very scary time because he could've been expelled. So please, do not copy someone else's work, and definitely don't copy from Wikipedia. Turnitin will know!

Group Study

Group studies are controversial in my worldview. I think they have the potential to be incredibly useful, but I'm a solitary learner and get more distracted than anything else if I'm studying around people. One really cool way that I participated in a group study once, though, was using Google Docs! A few of us in the class created a mutual Google document and shared it with one another. We used that to write important notes, ask questions, and help each other. I really liked that approach because I didn't have to physically be around other people while I was studying, but I was still able to tap into the supportive network we had built.

Independent Study

Doing an Independent Study is a great way of diving deep into a certain topic that may not be taught at your university. Throughout my time at university, I did three independent studies in three completely different departments (only one of them was in my major) and learnt so much! The first one was a project about the solar energy industry in the United States as compared to the rest of the world, with a special focus on United States' relationship with China. My second independent study was a project regarding American women in the political system and this turned into a research presentation at a conference! Finally, my last independent study was in my final semester and was about podcasting because I wanted to learn more about the industry as well as launch my own podcast!

All three of these independent studies gave me the opportunity to learn about topics that were not traditionally part of the curriculum. They were also opportunities to gain a more practical understanding of these issues or topics and create a holistic experiential learning experience. Finally, the third and most important aspect of doing an independent study is the one-on-one learning experience that is so valuable. I had the opportunity to spend an hour a week with a doctorate-holding expert, pick their brains about a topic they were passionate about, and avail myself of their guidance in exploring it for myself. The relationship you can build with a professor in this setting can be life-changing.

Meeting Deadlines

As a procrastinator, I can assure you that assignment deadlines are the only way I would ever get anything done. But, I figured out that if I had my assignment all planned out, it was much easier to be a procrastinator and still do very well, because even though I didn't start the final version before the day of submission, I had a great plan and knew exactly what I needed to write in the assignment. It saved me a lot of time, energy, and panic because while I work best under pressure, if I'm cutting it too close, I low-key panic about it.

A good way to go about planning an assignment is to divide it into parts and plan each part properly. This gives you the flexibility of finishing one part, then taking a break before you start the next. If you're a fellow procrastinator, you know that those breaks are key to our success.

Reward Yourself

Developing a reward system for yourself to encourage you to complete the task at hand can be very useful. This involves breaking up a big task into smaller steps or goals and then rewarding yourself at the completion of each one of those smaller steps or goals. For example, if I'm craving chips, I'll only allow myself to eat a couple after I'm done with each one of those steps. This helps me build self-discipline while accomplishing my goals.

Should You Take Classes with Friends?

I'm someone who loves to keep my social and academic lives separate. I enjoy becoming friends with my classmates, but I don't enjoy taking classes with close friends. I'm too much of a nerd bird and I try to be very focused during class. This is hard when I have a friend around me because I feel distracted and feel this weird need to talk to them. The worst-case scenario, though, is the awkwardness it creates if you and this friend stop being friends. Another weird scenario that is not as bad is if either you or your friend is doing extremely well in the class and the other is practically failing, it may result in group study sessions, which, when conducted with friends, never result in any real studying. So, now it won't just be the one friend doing poorly in the class but both of you, and that is *not* a healthy friendship.

Find Your Sweet Spot

It's a good idea to have a particular study spot, but I feel very hypocritical talking about this. I know very well that studying in bed is not the best idea, but more often than not, that's exactly what I do. The time when I studied in my bed the least was during my time at the University of Oxford, because the library culture is so huge there and I always felt very inspired when I was studying around other Oxford scholars. But, the reason you shouldn't study in bed is because it will either impact your studying habits negatively or your sleeping habits negatively. You may find yourself feeling tired and sleepy every time you begin to open a textbook or you may find yourself feeling very awake and focused at bedtime.

I try to stay awake until I'm falling asleep, so it's not that big of an issue for me, but I would still recommend having a study place that is separate from your bed. It can be a study table in your room or the library, or a study room in your dormitory building. But, pick wisely.

The Importance of Good Grades

In the American collegiate system, a 4.0 is a perfect score. In some countries, it may be 100 percent or something else.

As a first-year student, aiming for a 4.0 GPA is a great idea. However, if you're unable to achieve that, you mustn't beat yourself up about it. Your GPA is not the best predictor for your success in life; it is, however, an important tool that will help you go to a great graduate school if that is part of your plan. A high GPA shows that you are hardworking and disciplined, not necessarily extraordinarily intelligent. But, if you have a high GPA with great involvement and other experiences, it shows that you are a well-rounded individual who is ready to take on the real world!

What you should definitely *not* do, though, is base your identity on your GPA. I learnt this the hard way. Growing up, I was not the best student academically. I never enjoyed what I studied, and thus, did not apply myself to my maximum potential and never got the best grades. But when I came to university, I loved everything I was learning, and I was excelling at it. I had a 4.0 up until my second year, which was technically when I was a third-year student by credits, when my GPA dropped to a 3.96.

Now, that might not sound too scary to most people, but for a person who had based their identity on that 4.0 GPA, I was pretty upset in the beginning. But even so, I was not as upset as I expected myself to be. I received multiple pep talks (from others and myself; yes, I give myself motivational talks) about how I should not base my identity on a number, and it was then that I realised how we're taught very early on in our lives about how the numbers in our lives define us. Sometimes it can be your age or your weight, and very often, grades and test scores. It's never a bad idea to have big goals that include big numbers, but it's important that you don't allow the number to define you. You are more than just a number, and the fact of the matter is, the person who learnt the most will retain that information the most, not the one who was able to memorise and regurgitate the information for the purpose of that test or exam.

Homework

Homework sucks. I hated homework my entire school life and that didn't really change when I came to university. The good thing, though, was that it was very different from what I had traditionally viewed as homework. In my mind, homework is boring, mindless, and a complete waste of time. But assignments in university that required me to spend time on them outside the classroom were fun, enriching, and a completely valid use of my time. I felt intellectually empowered when I spent hours researching topics that I had no prior knowledge of and I loved it! While some classes did have some "homework," the professors did a really good job explaining the importance of doing it and why it would help us in the classroom. And I will be completely transparent and admit that I did not always complete my homework, but thankfully, there are several assignments that lead up to your final grade; not just one exam or some homework. The American class experience is very holistic and accommodates different learning styles and experiences.

Finals Week

"Home stretch" or "home straight" refers to the final time period before you are *done*. This can be done with a project or a rehearsal before a big performance, and in this context, it can be your semester. And what comes right before the end of the semester? FINALS!

Finals week can be stressful for many students, but it's important to remember that too much stress can interfere with your preparation, concentration, and your performance. It can lead to increased procrastination or setting unrealistic expectations—high or low—for yourself.

It's important to know what your personal stress buster is so that you have a plan in place if and when you feel stressed out. For me, hanging out with my friends, watching Netflix, or walking around the city while listening to music work extremely well. So, figure out your personal stress buster and make it part of your schedule during finals week.

In my opinion, the worst effect of stress is blanking out, when you forget what you have studied so meticulously at the most inopportune of times. This happens for one of three reasons: you didn't study enough, you didn't sleep enough, or you weren't motivated enough. Do you know what the common denominator in that situation is? It's YOU! So, if you make the right choices and study, sleep, and feel motivated, you won't forget what you've learnt and you will excel all your finals, whether they are projects, exams, or whatever!

Just the way you would set goals for the semester, set study goals for finals week and plan your schedule in advance. That way, you'll have a plan and you won't feel overwhelmed.

Additional Tips

Some tips for preparing for finals include prioritising difficult classes so that you can dedicate more time to them. Obviously, you're expected to know what material will be covered in the test; and if you don't, you can always check the syllabus or email your professor. If you're experiencing too much trouble with specific classes, you can avail yourself of tutoring services at the university or your professors' office hours. If you learn and focus better in group settings, you can certainly form study groups with classmates and friends. Figure out what works for YOU!

A big part of making sure that you're performing at a high level is to nourish your body. The top five brain foods include: nuts, fish, blueberries, dark chocolate, and whole grains. My favourite study food is dark chocolate covered almonds. So good!

While it's great to get a good night's rest before a big final, I fully expect you to be up studying or practicing and that's all right. I usually try to sleep and prefer waking up early the next morning to study or revise. Deep breathing and focused meditation will help you a ton with focus, concentration, and alleviating stress. And finally, talking to a close friend and just relaxing is very important so that you are in a positive mindset.

The day of the final, dress confidently, smile, and crush it! Trust me, *You Got This!*

Chapter 12

BEYOND ACADEMICS

As important as academics are to the university experience, involvement is just as important. I cannot imagine not having been involved during my time at university. I even made it a priority to be involved with organisations when I was studying abroad!

Think Broadly

One of the biggest pieces of advice I can give in terms of involvement is to be involved with organisations that are not directly related to your major. My involvement with UT Entrepreneurs opened so many doors for me that I don't know what I would've done without that organisation. It gave me friends, colleagues, and mentors; and as a Political

Science major, I was proof that it was an open and inclusive organisation for the entire student body. I have other friends who were part of the Sociology club or the Paintball club and LOVED their time around those who did not think like them, as did I. But of course, you should be involved with organisations that are connected to your major because those will open a whole other set of doors that you may not have access to without your involvement.

Boards

Another fun way to get involved with your university is to volunteer on student boards. The university's administration is constantly looking for students to serve on conduct or disciplinary boards, advisory boards, et cetera, because at the end of the day, only students can make the student experience better for themselves; not staff or faculty.

Competitions

Another cool way to get involved is by competing! Honestly, I'm not a big fan of competitions, but once in a while, I find myself wanting to get involved with an awesome competition. In my first semester of university I got involved with the Hult Prize competition. Though it was one of the first competitions I was to become involved with, it changed my life because it was this competition that introduced me to the idea of social entrepreneurship, the simple idea that one can start a business and make lots of money while still creating incredible impact in the community.

This is a very simple, yet profound, idea and I have been obsessed ever since. It's a critical component of who I am as an individual and the people I surround myself with. It's not controversial or illogical; all it takes for someone to understand it is a good explanation, and I have made it my mission to be an evangelist for this movement.

In fact, my academic career came full circle during my final year when I was selected to be the Campus Director for the Hult Prize at the University of Oxford. I have even created an interview-style show where I interview entrepreneurs and highlight their impact in the community. My journey with social entrepreneurship has been an interesting one because it started out with me telling everyone to be a social entrepreneur, but my message has now evolved into a cry to end social entrepreneurship. You can watch my TEDx talk to get a better understanding of why I say this, but simply stated, I believe that all entrepreneurship should be social entrepreneurship. We need to stop expecting companies to be socially responsible and instead expect it as a global norm.

Research

You can also become part of research projects with professors or other students, or even simply participate in others' projects. This will help you form strong relationships and help you to build your network. It can complement or supplement your classroom work. In fact, you can even convert that project into an independent study and get credit for completing it!

Media, Publications, and Student Government

I would highly recommend at least trying one of these to get a sense of patriotism towards your university and its community:

- Newspaper
- TV station
- Radio
- Annual Publication
- Student Government

I tried Student Government as a senator and had a wonderful experience. I also briefly worked with the newspaper and the

TV station which were both great experiences. The reason for this is, you get a whole new understanding and appreciation for the way things work at your university. You will also be in the know for most events and experiences that are being created. This is especially useful in a larger university where you may constantly feel like you have no idea what's going on because there is just so much going on!

Starting Your Own Organisation

Sometimes, no matter how many different organisations you try out, you just may not feel like you belong. You might feel like there just isn't one out there for you. But guess what? You have the ability to start your own organisation and build a community around something you feel strongly about. I was a founding member for a few different organisations and that was a very valuable experience! I felt like I was really impacting the university community and creating a network for similarly-minded individuals. Some of those worked and some of them didn't, but I am so proud of one of them in particular: co-founder of the ONE Campaign chapter at my university. That was singlehandedly one of the best experiences I had in those three years. My original co-founder graduated the semester after we started the organisation, but we remain close even today. The ONE Campaign is a non-profit that is very close to my heart and being involved with their efforts and being a champion for the cause has meant so much to me. I'll be telling you more about their amazing work in Part 3, but for now, let's focus on starting your own organisation.

Every university has a different policy on exactly how the process works, but a few important points to consider are:

- Is there a real need for this organisation?
- Will you be able to attract other students?

- Will you need to have staff or faculty on board?
- Do you have staff or faculty on board?
- Are you the right person with the right resources to make this work?
- Do you have the time to make this work?

The organisations that fail do so because they are unable to garner support. Most often, this support means attendance at events. Some schools tend to have a more active community than others, but don't let a less active community stop you. Starting something of your own and watching it work or fail will teach you things you cannot learn in a classroom, and I truly believe that it will make for a better overall university experience for you.

Sports

An important facet of American culture is sports. The country is *obsessed* with sports. Depending on the location of your university, the most popular or most watched sport may vary, but it's safe to say that by the end of your first semester, you will understand what the terms Super Bowl, Stanley Cup, and March Madness mean. And you will practically be *forced* to participate in the festivities of each of these regardless of your preference. It's just the American way of life. And honestly, it can be quite fun if you give it a chance. I mean, I have personally hoped that my friends would be just as excited about a La Liga or FIFA World Cup match, but that is not the American way of life, so unfortunately real football is not as big in the country. Oh wait, they don't even call it football—they call it soccer here. Ew. But I digress! Getting involved with sports is a great way to meet people and get more spirited about your university.

There are a few different ways for you to get involved with sports at your university. You can be on the official team and represent your university in state-wide or nation-wide competitions and such. There is ample funding for such programmes at most universities and you may even get scholarships for your tuition through your involvement with a sport. But this requires tons of commitment. You have to attend early morning practice, pick classes that work with your training schedule, miss classes to travel for matches, et cetera. Another option which is sport-specific is a club team. This is a more relaxed option and may not be available for every sport at your university. But at my university, for example, the ice hockey team was a club team, which meant that the players were part of a different governing organisation than the players of the baseball team. Finally, if you just want to play for fun, there's an American concept called "intramural sports," which is even more casual than the other two. Intramurals take place for a week or two every year (depending on your university) and students can form teams to compete in various sports. The winning team gets bragging rights, but everyone who takes part has tons of fun during this time. So, it's definitely a great option if you love playing a sport but cannot commit to spending too much time on it during the entire semester.

I personally was not involved with sports during my time at university but if you are someone who enjoys playing sports and the camaraderie that comes with it, I would highly recommend that you try it out!

Greek Life

Depending on the university you attend, Greek Life (fraternities and sororities) may be a big part of campus life. But, remember that visibility does not equate to action. I personally never felt compelled to be in a sorority because I am generally better with guy friends and it is expensive to be in a sorority. My thinking was that I didn't want to pay to be around people I wouldn't want to hang out with anyway.

Of course, that was *my* mindset; but if you are intrigued by Greek life, you should certainly try it out. Some of my most successful friends and students were part of Greek life and loved it. There is a network that those organisations provide access to and this can be very beneficial to your professional life—as long as you can put up with the parties and sometimes even hazing.

Don't Spread Yourself Too Thin

The big piece of caution with being involved is being *too* involved, which can really take a toll on your physical and mental health. If you don't already know your limit, in terms of how involved you can handle being, it's important to find out what your limit is. University is challenging as it is, and you do not want your fun involvement experiences to feel like work. I personally experienced burn out after being so deeply involved with so many different organisations, and I had to step down from some for my own sanity.

Take Full Advantage

Every university has opportunities that are specific to it. Sometimes, this may even be true for the programme you're in. Examples of these include study abroad opportunities, semester away programmes, and societies.

While your university may offer completely different opportunities, here are some examples from my university that can help you understand what to look for at yours.

At my university, there are several opportunities that are exclusive to Honors students. The most exclusive of these being the Oxford Study Abroad Programme. Each semester, the Honors department handpicks three students and sends them to the University of Oxford, and also pays for most of it. We only pay our regular tuition fees to the university and they cover the rest.

Another great opportunity is the Harvard National Model United Nations conference. This is a fully-paid trip that the Honors Program sponsors for the entire delegation from the university.

We also had an honours society called Phi Kappa Phi which is touted as America's oldest and most selective multidisciplinary collegiate honours society.

I was blessed to partake in all three of these amazing opportunities, but there were many others besides these.

There was the Washington Semester Program through the American University; there were several study abroad programmes, some of which were specific to different majors, and there were several scholarships, awards, and events.

It's important to pick a university with clout in the community because that opens so many doors for students. My university was located right in downtown Tampa and, while we had other universities in the city, we received more internship and job offers than the others, due to our location. The university also has a great reputation, which meant that we were able to go watch former U.S. President Barack Obama speak when he was in town. We hosted the incredible Randi Zuckerberg, founder of Facebook Live, and we have access to incredible individuals through the various boards and departments at the university.

Do Summer Right

Taking advantage of the summer is so important. Most of your peers will relax all summer and then realise that they're still stuck where they were before summer began. And that is NOT where you want to be.

The best way to have a productive summer is to continue to stay in the momentum of your regular terms but giving yourself the ability to relax a little bit. Because rest and relaxation are very important for ensuring that you don't burn out.

If you're studying in America, taking classes at your university or at a community college can help you tremendously in terms of getting ahead and being able to graduate early. More often than not, community colleges tend to be less expensive and also more flexible. Some even offer 100 percent online classes! Just make sure to get approval from your university beforehand and you'll be set.

Another productive option is internships or other work experience that will give you a feel of the real world and some money to spend when the semester rolls in. Part 3 will focus more on internships and jobs and how you can find them, so I won't go into detail about it now. It is important to remember, though, that if you're doing it for credit, you need to pay your university for those credits. Also, if you're an international student, you have to take it for at least 1 credit (it could be more depending on your university's policies), but it does have to be for academic credit to be safe from a legal standpoint.

If you love travelling, then make travel a key element of your summer. I personally love travelling, and while I travel during the terms as well, I don't have the opportunity to travel as often as I can when I have to be in class. So, make the most of this break and travel to new places, old favourites, and just go explore! Travelling will teach you things no classroom ever could, and that type of learning is just as important as your traditional classroom learning experience.

Finally, if you plan to stay in the city or town of your university after graduation, I would highly recommend staying there at least for one entire summer so that you're exposed to what normal life looks like in that place. And chances are that you'll either love it and know for sure that you want to really live there, or you may realise that it's not meant to be. My personal experience was a mix of both because I love Tampa, but the summers are much slower-paced than the rest of the year and it's very hot, so I would like to travel to other places during the summer.

Studying Abroad

As I mentioned earlier in the book, my entire university experience was a study abroad experience because I'm from India and I got my degree from the University of Tampa in the United States. Given this context, while I was interested in studying abroad through my university, there was only one programme that I was *really* interested in. This was the most exclusive opportunity offered at my university and I had my eyes set on it since my first week of classes. This was the opportunity to study at the University of Oxford through the Honors Program. So, when the time came, I was ready to rock my application and my interview, and I had spent countless hours researching what I wanted to study and get involved with there.

On the day of my interview with the Honors faculty committee, I was very confident in myself. I walked in and shook all twelve of their hands and presented each one of them with a copy of a résumé that I had created just for this interview. I had been told by many students and faculty members that most people do not get selected on their first attempt, but I was determined. I rocked my interview and felt really good about it. A week later, when I received the news that I had been selected, I was ecstatic! I knew I had worked hard for this for almost two years and I had not allowed myself to waver from that goal.

Studying abroad at Oxford was magical. I get asked about the experience on an almost daily basis, and the closest answer to how I truly feel is that it was magical. Don't get me wrong, Tampa is magical in its own right and is still my most favourite place in the entire world. Oxford is just magical in a very different and very real sense. The architecture, the history, and its prominence in the making of the world as we know it is so real. Each nook and corner has a story, and I thoroughly enjoyed that. My favourite thing about Oxford, the university and the city, was that social entrepreneurship was the norm. The conversation did not revolve around, "What is it?" It revolved around, "What more can we do?" That made my heart so happy.

So, would I recommend studying at Oxford? Yes! Academically, there are few places on the planet that can even come close to the prestige behind the Oxford brand. The academic experience there is very different from the American university experience and my experience reaffirmed my belief that I want to pursue a graduate degree and become Dr. Juhi!

I don't think I would have enjoyed it as much if I had chosen to study in England for my entire undergraduate education because changing your major is not really a thing in England or Asia. Liberal Arts is almost non-existent in those places. There, you choose a discipline and study it intently for three years without really experiencing other disciplines; and given that I initially wanted to major in Psychology, I would have been miserable if I'd been stuck with only studying that for my entire undergraduate experience.

To create a successful study abroad experience for myself, I followed all the approaches I've already listed in the book. In fact, that's what reaffirmed my belief that I should write this book because while a good majority of it is based on my time in the American university system as an international student, there's a lot in here that can be applied to a university experience almost anywhere.

The big tip would be to focus on having fun while not ignoring your academic responsibilities. I say this because studying abroad is a once-in-a-lifetime opportunity that you should take full advantage of. It's not often in life that you'll be able to fully immerse yourself in a different culture with minimal responsibilities. I most certainly took advantage of every opportunity that came my way and tried new things, kept up my skills and passions for things I was already interested in, and travelled as much as I could!

If you choose to study abroad at the University of Oxford, I would highly recommend going through the Oxford Study Abroad Programme (OSAP) because the people at OSAP are phenomenal. The team works tirelessly doing whatever they possibly can to ensure that every single term, every single student has the best time at Oxford. Oh and, they have the sweetest dog as an office dog. Her name is Bella, and my time there would not have been the same without her!

Part 3

LANDING

Chapter 13

CRAFTING A PROFESSIONAL IMAGE

I am a major advocate of not allowing other people's opinions to affect my personal life; but in the real world, your professional image is only as good as someone else says or thinks it is. Therefore, it's very important to carefully craft an appealing and flattering image that, to a large extent, can be controlled.

So, what's the difference between your professional image and your personal image?

Professional Image

In the time we're living now, it's very hard to distinguish between the two because our society is so focused on identity. It's almost impossible to separate your professional image from your personal image. This means that your professional image includes how you appear in person, over the phone, via text and email, and even on the internet.

A study conducted by researchers at the Albert Ludwigs University of Freiburg found that it only takes a few milliseconds for us to make subconscious judgments about the people we meet. While it's easier to manage your first physical impression by embracing style and etiquette tips, it's much harder to manage one's online or any other type of impression. This is why it's important that everything you post (or that is posted about you) is in a positive light. While critics will emerge as soon as you start gaining internet influence, it's rather smart to ensure that those drunk photos do not get posted on Facebook.

First Step to Success

A major element of your professional image is showing up. Not how you look when you show up, but the fact that you do. A motto that I hold close is, "Showing up is the first step to success" and the person who said this to me was a professor at my university. The context in which he said this to me was when we were boarding a bus to go on a day trip to a conference in Orlando. About 50 students had signed up. Considering this, the university had arranged for a large bus to take us to the event and bring us back. On this cold Saturday morning, there were maybe 13 of us ready to go at 8:00 in the morning and most of the others were graduating seniors who were trying to bump up their résumés.

Me? I was just an overly enthusiastic freshman who couldn't pass up an opportunity to learn about something she didn't know anything about, in this case, finance. But the biggest payoff I had from attending this event was getting into the professor's good books and meeting Keith (who is one of my closest friends, even today). By choosing to show up on that cold (as cold as Florida can be) Saturday morning to attend an event that most of the registrants had chosen not to attend, I was able to gain lots of brownie points with the professor; and although he wasn't *my* professor, I was able to leverage that connection when I needed something done.

Later that year, I wanted to take a 300-level Entrepreneurship class without having taken a single business class in my life, and he was able to help me make that happen. But, consistency is important. By taking this class and getting an A in it as the only Freshman, I was able to show him that I was truly motivated and hardworking, and his efforts had not been wasted. This is how I was able to keep up my first impression with him.

Best Thing You Could Wear

For better or worse, you are going to be judged based on what you wear. And the most important thing you could wear is a smile. A study conducted by Kelton Global reported that participants rated a smile as more important than the spoken word when it came to first impressions. This can relate to your in-person appearance as well as photos on social media. Pouting and smouldering may be in vogue and it may look sexy, but photos of you smiling will get the most positive professional reception overall.

Online Image

It's also important to keep in mind that while you may proactively keep your social media "clean," other people in your life might not be on the same page. Some people are way too focused on posting every photo, regardless of how flattering or unflattering it may be, so it's important for you to ensure that you untag or ask your friends to remove photos that may show you in an unappealing light.

Another big one is photos and videos of you engaging in illegal activities. As one of my friends puts it, "Rule number 1 of doing illegal things is to not post photos of yourself doing it on social media." And while it may seem harmless at the time, it can have major consequences on your academic and professional life.

A few years ago, a popular YouTube channel sent a film crew to Tampa to cover the annual Gasparilla festival. The crew filmed a video with students drinking and engaging in commonplace drunk college student behaviour, but the video's viral status resulted in my university finding out. Given that most of the students were under 21, it was illegal for them to have been drinking, and given that it was all on film, the university expelled every student that could be identified. So, no. Posting that picture of yourself chugging that beer is *not* a good idea.

Google Yourself

Lastly, something else that you should do to ensure your online presence is strong and positive is to Google yourself periodically. First, ensuring that there is nothing crazy showing up when someone types your name; and second, ensuring that you are showing up when someone types your name. If you have an uncommon name, chances are your social media accounts will show up on the first page of the search results, but if you have a relatively common name, you need to make sure that you show up at least for specific keywords like your location or area of interest.

Additional Tips

In terms of your in-person image, remember Oscar Wilde and the first half of his over-used quote, "You can never be overdressed or overeducated." Body language is important, so smile and stand (or sit up) straight. Always shake hands properly and make eye contact with the person you're talking to. In terms of texting or emailing, the #GrammarNazi inside me will tell you that you should write in full sentences and use appropriate punctuation marks. I am personally very wary of people who do not use correct grammar over text and email. There are some words and phrases that I am more lax about, but if u type lyk dis, derz a v high chance dat i will nt respnd 2 u.

Chapter 14:

BUILDING YOUR PERSONAL BRAND

Your professional image is an extension of your personal brand. Your brand is who you project yourself to be, and your image is who people perceive you to be. This is why it's so important to be consistent and aim for a positive brand as well as a positive professional image.

One thing that really helped me build my personal brand was to outline who I wanted to be. I wrote down all the qualities and areas that I wanted to be known for (or in) and then backtracked to what my current status was, so I could map out how I could get to where I wanted to be. This is a form of goal setting and was an extension of my overall goal setting process.

It's one thing to create your personal brand for yourself, but it's another to communicate it effectively. The communication process is multifaceted. Here's how I went about it.

Dress the Part

The first thing I did was dress the part. While other students were going to class in their pyjamas, starting my second semester I was dressing in business casual. This is not to say that you need to spend hundreds of dollars on suits, you just need to buy the right clothes when you are shopping.

As I said, your appearance is a very important part of your image and can either make you memorable or forgettable. A friend of mine was known as "the guy in the suit" even to people who didn't personally know him. He wore a suit every single day and people noticed. He was always looked at in a different way. In my case, instead of dressing in crop tops and bathing suits to class (yes, I have personally witnessed that), I was wearing dresses and blazers; and again, people noticed.

One day, I was dressed very casually and getting a smoothie on campus and some random girl stopped me and commented on how she didn't think I even owned casual clothes because she had never once seen me in anything other than formal wear. Even professors have commented on how I always came across as 'put together' because of the way I dress. I can assure you that I was *not* always 'put together'. But when someone thinks you are, they are more likely to make exceptions for you when you need them to because they do not think of you as a bum. Again, this is not to say that everyone should be walking around in suits; but dress the way the people you want to connect with will respect. If you are an athlete, you will dress differently than someone who is an aspiring businessperson and vice versa. Your clothes send a strong message about how you carry yourself and have a major effect on people's perceptions of who you are, be that colleagues and classmates or professors and staff.

Business Cards

The next thing I did was to have business cards made. Below is an image of my first business card ever, and while there are lots of things I would change about it now, it did its job back then. It was vertically laid out, so it was different. It had all my important information, so that was useful; and it had a quote about me from a reputable source, so it gave me credibility that, as a second-year college student, is relatively uncommon to have.

Juhi Kore

"AN ENTHUSIASTIC, ENERGETIC, AND PASSIONATE SPEAKER"[1]

PUBLIC SPEAKING
ENTREPRENEURSHIP
WORLD AFFAIRS

JUHI.KORE@SPARTANS.UT.EDU
813.943.2507
LINKEDIN.COM/IN/JUHIKORE

"AND I— I TOOK THE ONE LESS TRAVELED BY"

WWW.JUHIKORE.COM

[1] JULIANE MORA, PHD

A lot of people in my "real world" circles were very impressed that I had business cards. My biggest reason for even getting them was that I was tired of always being the one reaching out. Whenever I attended an event and met real people there, they would always hand me their business cards and ask me to reach out. But after I got my business cards and was able to reciprocate their gesture, I could ask them to reach out to me, and more often than not, they did!

Website

The third thing I did was to create a personal website. While it's not mandatory to purchase your own domain, I highly recommend doing so if you're planning to position yourself as a public figure. If your name is already taken, try 'the<fullname>.com' or '<field><firstname>.com' or something else that has your name and your area of expertise or interest. But, regardless of whether you buy a domain or create a free WordPress website, having something is key. It can seem like a daunting task, and if you are anything like me, you'll be worried that it isn't perfect, but I want to assure you that that's *okay*. The goal is to release an MVP (Minimum Viable Product) and then work on it behind the scenes. There are so many templates available online, but you can use mine as a guideline.

LinkedIn

Next, I curated and updated my profile on LinkedIn. Given that I was involved with over 100 different activities in just two years of university, it was impossible to add everything to my profile. But I did add my official jobs and positions and my honours and awards while also creating a bio that included just enough information to get someone interested in looking at the rest of my profile. As part of my on-campus job as a Career Ambassador, I was given an in-depth training into LinkedIn, and I'm going to share some insights from that with you in the upcoming chapter focused on the LinkedIn platform.

Elevator Pitch

Finally, the last thing I did for my personal brand was have the right elevator pitch for the different situations and people I would encounter. Given that the top three things I was passionate about were speaking, social entrepreneurship, and international relations, I had one general elevator pitch that covered all of them, and then specific pitches for each. The important point is to make sure you know the end goal before you start the conversation. Are you looking for a job opportunity? An internship? A connection? A meeting? Once you have that figured out, it's much easier to outline and plan your elevator pitch. Before I tell you what my elevator pitch generally sounds like, let me tell you more about what an elevator pitch is and what it should include.

An elevator pitch is traditionally a 90-second speech (pitch) about yourself, or in business situations, about your company that can help you sell either yourself or an idea to someone during an elevator ride. While 90 seconds is the traditional time limit, you have to engage someone in the first 10 seconds so that they even care about the rest. So, it's very important for an elevator pitch to start off in a very engaging manner. Similar to a normal speech, you need to establish a connection or build some sort of relationship with your audience, even if that audience is just one person. An anecdote or a compliment works very well for starting a conversation that leads to an elevator pitch.

The best part about elevator pitches is that they almost never actually take place in an elevator, thus taking some of the pressure off of you. It just needs to be succinct and cover the basics of what someone would need to know in order to want to know more. It is a little like a trailer for the movie that is your life. It needs to be interesting and informative, while still keeping things intriguing so that the other person(s) wants to either continue the conversation or schedule a follow-up call or meeting. This is why you don't want to give away too much, because then the other person might feel like they already know everything there is to know about you or your company and won't want to spend more time getting to know it (or you) better.

Personal Elevator Pitch outline:
    Establish connection!
    Who are you?
    Who are they?
    Why you?
    Next step?

My Personal Elevator Pitch

"Hey, I just heard you talking about social impact and I would love to introduce myself to you! I'm Juhi and I study Political Science and Leadership Studies at the University of Tampa. I am very passionate about social entrepreneurship and I believe that it is going to solve every global problem we have. I heard you work for XYZ charity and I love the work it does for underprivileged children in our city. I would love to chat more with you about adopting a social enterprise mindset for your charity so that you can make your organisation more sustainable without relying on donations and grants. I have worked with several social enterprises in the area and I'd love to get your contact information, so we can schedule a follow-up phone call or meeting. What do you say?"

Company/Idea Elevator Pitch outline:
    Problem?
    Solution!
    Why you?
    Next step?

Company/Idea Elevator Pitch Example

"Don't you hate the weather in this city? One minute it's too cold and the other it's unbearably hot. I used to spend hours deciding what to wear and no matter what I picked, I would still have the same problem. Fortunately, I was not the only one with this problem and so I got together with some of my buddies and we have created the brand-new ABC jacket which has an inbuilt intelligent heating and cooling system! The jacket is connected to your phone's weather app and can track the temperature and keep you at your selected temperature all the time. There are some other jackets like this in the market, but ours is the most affordable and ethically-sourced one out there. Would you like to try it for yourself?"

Just like any other type of speech, you need to practice your elevator pitch to get it perfect. The best part about your elevator pitch is that you can practice it anywhere and with anyone, because it is meant to be more general and rather quick. Once you've prepared an elevator pitch, you can go to different networking events like career fairs, recruitment events, and even social events. You can learn more about that in the upcoming chapter about Networking.

Chapter 15

THE 4 ESSENTIAL ELEMENTS

The Indispensable Résumé

Once you know what you want your professional image and your personal brand to look like, you need to relay this effectively to other people that you might want to work for or collaborate with. A résumé is a tool designed to do just that.

The résumé is a tool that allows you to showcase yourself and all the work you have done that is most relevant to the opportunity you're seeking. While I will talk about all the important sections in further detail, it primarily includes your education, work experience, skills, and honours. Just like the elevator pitch is a trailer to your life, think about the résumé as the highlight reel for the football game that is your life! Oh and, I mean *real* football, not American football! But I digress! Remember, your résumé needs to project *you* as the perfect candidate for the job! This is why it is of utmost importance to tailor your résumé to every single job you apply for.

In 2012, an IBM executive was quoted saying that about 90 percent of all big companies use software programmes to screen candidates and their résumés, and that it would be almost impossible to find a Fortune 500 company that did not use one of these programmes. Less than half of all recruiting managers even read a few of the résumés they receive, so rest assured, it's extremely likely that you will be screened by a machine, not a human. These tracking programmes that screen résumés for potential candidates are programmed to grade a résumé in terms of certain keywords, former employers, including the academic as well as professional experiences of the candidate. Often, low-scoring candidates won't even make it to the interview round. This is why it's important to place exact keywords from the job description into your résumé so that the software will pick out the words and give you a higher score.

Another way to get a better sense of what you actually need to include in your résumé is to check the website and social media accounts of the company and look for words and phrases that may indicate the company's mission, vision, and culture as these may not be in the job description but can still be in the software's programming. Another important tip for ensuring your résumé doesn't get tossed away is to not exceed 1-2 sides. In most cases, try your best to stick to 1 side, unless you are explicitly asked to send over a longer résumé. Recruiters spend an average of 30 seconds on each résumé, so make sure you have all your important details on the first (and preferably only) side.

Also, unless you're applying for a purely creative or design-focused opportunity, keep it simple! In terms of keeping it simple, remember that consistency of format is key. I almost lost an opportunity that was created specifically for me because my would-be boss thought my overly creative nature might overshadow what was needed to be accomplished. He basically thought I was too focused on design and creativity, and that focus could hamper the bigger goals he wanted me to accomplish. It took some convincing, but I was finally able to show him that I had my priorities straight.

Placing keywords into your résumé is a general tip, but what else do you actually include? What should be the substantive elements of your résumé?

Well, let's analyse the résumé below.

Mickey McPherson
Lalaland, XY 34341
Nutritionist | Fitness Coach | Researcher
linkedin.com/mickeymp

+1 (321) 123-3120   mickeymp@email.com

EDUCATION

Bachelor of Science in Nutrition Science (Honors)   May 2018
Minors in Leadership Studies and Physiology   Lalaland, XY, U.S.A.
The University of Lalaland
GPA: 3.59 – Working part-time while attending university

Honors & Awards: Dean's List, Academic Research Award 2016, Johnson Scholarship Award, Bob Bobby Outstanding First Year of Involvement Award, Leadership and Academic Achievement Award, Student Leader of the Month, Athletics Fellowship 2017

EXPERIENCE

Organiser & Facilitator   February 2018-April 2018
Annual Athletic Summit   Lalaland, XY
- Worked directly with sponsors and exhibitors to ensure a smooth sailing logistical process for this year's premier athletic event
- Advised on marketing strategy, exhibitor coordination and directly supervised over 500 sponsorship relationships
- Facilitated a workshop about nutrition and weight loss and helped the audience create detailed nutrition plans

Campus Director   September 2017-Present
Althlex Prize at University of Lalaland   Lalaland, XY
- Organised logistics and operations and pitched the event for $1,450 in sponsorship acquisition
- Selected and finalised teams, mentors, and judges for the event
- Worked with 15 teams and taught them the Lean Bean Machine method of food science

Vice President   March 2016-Present
Nutritionists of the Future at University of Lalaland   Lalaland, XY
- Improved membership of a dying on-campus organisation by 300% and implemented a brand new mentorship programme
- Worked with aspiring nutritionists to demonstrate and refine the entrepreneurial process and pitch coaching for finals
- Oversaw logistics and operations for all the meetings in 2016 & 2017

Operations Intern   December 2015-June 2016
Nutri Education   Lalaland, XY
- Secured meetings with potential investors and partners all over the world and built effective relationships on behalf of the team
- Created highly detailed instructional manuals and impact models for the early childhood nutrition company
- Mentored and facilitated the on-boarding training of new interns

ACADEMIC EXPERIENCE

NSC 450 – Advanced Food Chemistry   Spring 2018
    Lalaland, XY
- Learned about advanced food processing techniques and the intersection of technology and gastronomy
- Analysed the principles of new gastronomy and their practical usage and implementation in developing fusion-style cuisines
- Examined and studied Kent Robertson's "Main Approach to Gastronomical Development" and discussed its implementation and practicality in modern cuisine restaurants

NSC 443 – Advanced Human Physiology   Fall 2017
    Lalaland, XY
- Gained a deep understanding of the nine human organ systems
- Analysed the up and coming research in human physiology and conducted primary research to test out theories
- Worked collaboratively in a 5 person team to present advanced understanding of human cardiovascular system

SKILLS

- Proficient in Python and Java Script programming languages
- Strong research and writing skills demonstrated by participation and presentations at national conferences
- Multilingual with fluency in English, Spanish, and Hebrew

Your name must be in bold and centred at the very top of your résumé. The font size for your name should be larger by a point or two. In this example, the contact information is all on one line, because there is a lot of substantive content in the other sections of the résumé, but if you don't have enough content to fill up an entire page, feel free to rearrange the contact information to cover more lines. Get rid of the words *phone* and *email* and just have your number and email address on there. Make sure you use a custom LinkedIn URL, and that your email address is professional and simple. If you have certain keywords as part of your personal brand, you can put those here as well.

Mickey McPherson
+1 (321) 123-3120   Lalaland, XY 34341   mickeymp@email.com
Nutritionist | Fitness Coach | Researcher
linkedin.com/mickeymp

An optional section between your information and your first main section is a summary or an objective statement. A summary is a short paragraph about your interest in the opportunity, while an objective statement is a straightforward one-liner about the opportunity. The example does not include this, but an objective statement would be something like:

> "Highly-motivated Political Science student looking for Urban Development Intern position at XYZ Urban Development Group."

A summary, on the other hand, would be a little more detailed and will go something like:

> "Highly-motivated and passionate student with leadership and research experience looking for Urban Development Intern position at XYZ Urban Development Group to learn about the industry and develop further skills and knowledge in urban development and urban planning."

As a college student, the most recent and important aspect about you is your education, so the first category should be your educational background. If you are a first-year student, you can include your high school information as well, but second-year and after, your college information will suffice.

Additionally, make sure to include your full degree, any minors, expected date of graduation, and your GPA if it's above 3.5 out of 4. If it's lower than that, but you've been playing a sport consistently or have been working full-time or part-time, you can put that down next to your GPA as well, so as to showcase yourself as a well-rounded student. Finally, you can mention any honours and scholarships you have received during your time at university. Again, unless you are a first-year student, don't mention any high school era honours.

EDUCATION
Bachelor of Science in Nutrition Science (Honors) May 2018
Minors in Leadership Studies and Physiology Lalaland, XY, U.S.A.
The University of Lalaland
GPA: 3.59 – Working part-time while attending university

Honors & Awards: Dean's List, Academic Research Award 2016, Johnson Scholarship Award, Bob Bobby Outstanding First Year of Involvement Award, Leadership and Academic Achievement Award, Student Leader of the Month, Athletics Fellowship 2017

When it comes to the experience section, there are lots of ways to approach it. Depending on the opportunity you're applying for, you can categorise your experience into different sections. Remember, experience doesn't have to mean *paid* experience. It can include unpaid internships or on-campus experiences as well! If the description says they're looking for someone with leadership experience and software programming experience, you can create two separate headings and include your experiences in those two areas. If you don't have enough experience for multiple headings, you can call it relevant experience and put everything under that.

Note that it's best to list your experience entries in reverse chronological order. This puts your most recent experience at the top. Various categories of experiences you can include are class projects, internships, volunteer work, research projects, organisational activities, and any jobs you might have had. If you're trying to fill up space and have some experience that might not be directly related, you can create another heading called Additional or Other Experience and write down the experience without really expanding on it. Simply include the job title, company name, start and end dates, and location.

The bullet points for your experience entries must be well-crafted with keywords and action verbs that will be rated highly by the software screening programme and convey your skills effectively. While creating your bullet points, make sure you have the job description in front of you and that you make note of each and every skill mentioned in the description. Once you have noted them, think about which ones you have and which ones you don't. Highlight the ones you have and circle the ones you don't. This should give you a good idea as to whether or not you should even be applying for this position because if you have more circled skills than highlighted ones, you won't have a high chance of getting the opportunity, and even if you get it, you may not be able to do a good job at it.

When crafting each bullet point, you must make sure to keep the sentences succinct, yet descriptive. No one is going to want to read a long paragraph about your time as an intern at a law firm; they simply want to know what skills you gained and how much impact you created. This is why I urge you to use lots of action verbs and numbers in the bullet points. You need to craft your bullet points to begin with action verbs that convey the specific skill you have learnt and then include specific numbers so that you gain more credibility. Whenever possible, give exact numbers to represent the impact you created in your role because people tend to take candidates that can measure their impact more seriously.

EXPERIENCE

Organiser & Facilitator — February 2018-April 2018
Annual Athletic Summit — Lalaland, XY
- Worked directly with sponsors and exhibitors to ensure a smooth sailing logistical process for this year's premier athletic event
- Advised on marketing strategy, exhibitor coordination and directly supervised over 500 sponsorship relationships
- Facilitated a workshop about nutrition and weight loss and helped the audience create detailed nutrition plans

Campus Director — September 2017-Present
Althlex Prize at University of Lalaland — Lalaland, XY
- Organised logistics and operations and pitched the event for $1,450 in sponsorship acquisition
- Selected and finalised teams, mentors, and judges for the event
- Worked with 15 teams and taught them the Lean Bean Machine method of food science

Vice President — March 2016-Present
Nutritionists of the Future at University of Lalaland — Lalaland, XY
- Improved membership of a dying on-campus organisation by 300% and implemented a brand new mentorship programme
- Worked with aspiring nutritionists to demonstrate and refine the entrepreneurial process and pitch coaching for finals
- Oversaw logistics and operations for all the meetings in 2016 & 2017

Operations Intern — December 2015-June 2016
Nutri Education — Lalaland, XY
- Secured meetings with potential investors and partners all over the world and built effective relationships on behalf of the team
- Created highly detailed instructional manuals and impact models for the early childhood nutrition company
- Mentored and facilitated the on-boarding training of new interns

ACADEMIC EXPERIENCE

NSC 450 – Advanced Food Chemistry — Spring 2018
Lalaland, XY
- Learned about advanced food processing techniques and the intersection of technology and gastronomy
- Analysed the principles of new gastronomy and their practical usage and implementation in developing fusion-style cuisines
- Examined and studied Kent Robertson's "Main Approach to Gastronomical Development" and discussed its implementation and practicality in modern cuisine restaurants

NSC 443 – Advanced Human Physiology — Fall 2017
Lalaland, XY
- Gained a deep understanding of the nine human organ systems
- Analysed the up and coming research in human physiology and conducted primary research to test out theories
- Worked collaboratively in a 5 person team to present advanced understanding of human cardiovascular system

Your skills section is for hard skills only. Soft skills must be conveyed through the bullet points that you use to describe your experiences. Hard skills include languages, computer programmes relevant to your industry, technical skills, or any specific certifications. Remember to also list your proficiency levels when you list these skills.

SKILLS
- Proficient in Python and Java Script programming languages
- Strong research and writing skills demonstrated by participation and presentations at national conferences
- Multilingual with fluency in English, Spanish, and Hebrew

Some general tips include avoiding the mention of any religious or political affiliations unless that is the type of sector you are looking to be part of. You're also not required to mention your birthday or include photographs of yourself unless specifically asked to do so. Do not use an overly creative font type and certainly don't use an extremely small or extremely large font size. My personal favourite is Times New Roman at 10 for all résumés.

Overall, résumés are very subjective and it's always best to check with the people you are submitting the résumé to for specific guidelines, but all the tips here have been gathered from recruiters and other career services professionals and will be a great starting point for you to create your own résumé.

Cover Letter: A Résumé's Best Friend

I find cover letters very interesting because they're not as detailed or as formal as résumés, but they're just as important! Cover letters allow you to showcase a more personal side of yourself to your potential employer. But remember, just as with résumés, you'll have to send out customised cover letters to gain any semblance of real traction and interest. If possible, you could even write the letter by hand, but if you do, please make sure that your handwriting is legible.

In terms of the header format, keep it consistent with your résumé header. This reinforces your name and information in their mind.

The cover letter answers three main questions:
Why Them?
Why You?
What's Next?

Let's dive a little deeper into that.

Why Them?

This is what you answer first and foremost, because let's be real, nobody cares about you; they only care about themselves. Where most applicants might start their letter by talking about how they're the perfect candidate for the position, you can differentiate yourself by focusing on the company or the person. This will immediately grab their attention and also show them that you have researched their company (or them as an individual) and are genuinely interested in them. Make sure to include words from their mission and vision and why you would like to work for them.

Why You?

Now that you've tooted their horn a little bit, you can talk about yourself. But again, everything you say about yourself should be a reflection of how *they* would benefit. When you talk about a skill or quality that you possess, talk about why that would be useful in the position that you're looking for. Also, don't reiterate the same skills and qualifications that you have on your résumé. Make sure that it contains different information. Remember, the cover letter is a complement to the résumé, so it's okay to add more detail to specific items from your résumé and add more of a human or personal touch to it, but don't restate the same information in the exact same way.

What's Next?

This is probably the most overlooked part of the résumé on behalf of the position seeker. Most people end their cover letters with a simple, "Thank you for your time," or "I look forward to hearing from you." You need to be bold and action-oriented to see real results! Instead of a cliché ending, add something along the lines of, "I look forward to following up with you about this opportunity next week." This shows that you are confident and very serious about this opportunity.

Finally, add a signature. You can either scan your own handwriting or digitally add your signature to it through programmes like Preview on the macOS.

Who Can Vouch for You?

A reference list is usually submitted in conjunction with a résumé and cover letter. It lists the name and contact information of about 3-5 individuals who can vouch for you professionally, and their relationship to you.

So, remember, while your mum may say lots of kind things about you, she is *not* a good reference unless you have worked for her in a professional setting. Even in that case, it's best to leave your mum out of the picture.

Your reference list can include professors, colleagues, supervisors, and former employers. The most important part is to let them know that they are on your reference list. You most certainly don't want a potential employer to call someone you have on your list only to have them not remember you or not having anything substantive to say about you. I once applied for a speaking opportunity and listed the different things I was involved with that were proof of my expertise in the topic. Little did I know, the person evaluating my form was checking with other people that were involved with one of the community organising events I had listed, and fortunately, the person he reached out to knew me and my work and my experience and vouched for me. But had I just listed something I was not fully invested in, I probably would not have received a strong recommendation.

So, after you add someone to your list and tell them that they are on your list, also give them an idea of what to say. Be specific about the opportunity you're applying for and maybe even give them a copy of your résumé and highlight what you would like them to touch upon if they are contacted.

In terms of format, keep the heading consistent with the résumé and cover letter. As for the references themselves, this is a good template:

> John Doe
> Internship Supervisor at XYZ Ltd.
> 723 W Allison Blvd,
> Tampa FL 33701
> 813-123-1234
> John.doe@xyz.com

Recommendation Letters

Recommendation letters are mostly required for academic opportunities, and your best bet is a professor you may have worked closely with or whose class you did very well in. Again, the rule of thumb is to make sure they know what the opportunity is and what you want them to highlight. You may not always be privy to their final version of the letter, but you can have a good idea of what's in it beforehand if you have provided them with all the pertinent information. So, it's crucial that you pick someone who has lots of great things to say about you and who you can trust to vouch for you. Any sort of hesitation on their part is a sign that they won't be the best person to write it and you should look for someone else.

A big part of getting good references and recommendation letters is to never burn any bridges. Even if you don't like your previous employer or internship supervisor, make sure you still have a decent relationship with them. Lots of industries have a small number of key people, and if you are in the bad books of one, chances are you'll be in the bad books of many others. You really don't want to have a bad reputation before you even start being a real person.

Another is to be memorable wherever you go. Being memorable goes a long, long way. Whether it's your humour, age, personality, or a quirk, try your best to be memorable. I'm constantly remembered as the young girl who's in love with the city of Tampa. While that's not all there is to me, it still helps that people remember me as that person. Don't try to be someone you're not and don't try too hard to be funny or intelligent. Be who you are and let that shine through. *You Got This!*

Chapter 16

NETWORKING

Networking is an extremely important part of being a successful student and "real person." Two of my favourite quotes about networking are, "You are the sum of the five people you hang out with the most" and "Your network determines your net worth." If the idea of networking scares you, don't think of it as networking. Think of it more as connecting with awesome people and building real friendships and relationships, because that is what any good networker does.

In order of importance, I would rank the three elements of networking as follows:

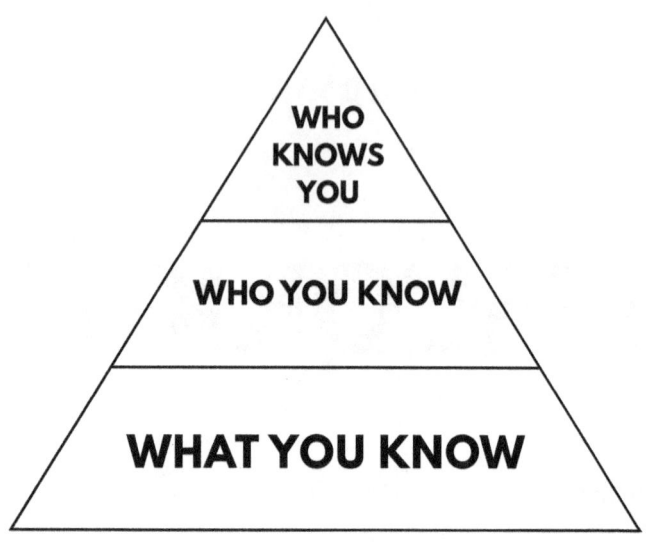

This is because, while what you know is important in building your base, through your personal, academic or professional background, you will gain a base of people around you based on what and who you are. But after that, you will need to get access to the right people, and this is where it comes in handy to have the right people know you.

Don't Forget the Ones You Already Know

The basics of this is reaching out to people you already know. This includes your family and friends, colleagues and classmates, and even professors. But the next step is getting these people who know you to reach out to other people on your behalf. Unless someone knows you and has a relationship of trust built with you, they will not vouch for you. This isn't because they're not helpful, it's because, if anything were to go wrong, they'll be the ones who will pay the price, and quite understandably. If someone is going out on a limb to do you a favour, you'd better make it worth their effort!

One thing to consider when trying to connect with someone outside of your circle is to first look for connections inside your circle. We often forget that the people in our lives have lives outside of our relationship bubble with them. What I mean by that is, if you have a friend at the gym, that friend knows people outside of the gym, too. They have a family, a professional life, et cetera.

Networking Events

A big part of today's professional culture is networking events. While I'm not the biggest fan of these events, there is some value to them if you go about it the right way. The first thing is to talk to new people.

"What? Of course, Juhi! I am going to a networking event to meet new people!"

While most people think it's fairly obvious that you need to go talk to people at the event, they often end up only talking to people they already know. This can be the friend(s) they went with, the friends they usually run into, or the friends they haven't seen in a long time. Instead of treating the event as a hangout session with the people you already know, treat it like a hangout session with people you *don't* know. This mindset will make you feel more comfortable and encourage you to meet new people and kindle real friendships, not just half-baked acquaintanceship.

Whatever you do, *do not* be the person who hands their business card to every person at the event and exchanges not a word more than, "Hi, my name is John Doe. Please reach out to me!" That is the worst form of an elevator pitch you could have and is one of my biggest pet peeves. It's much better to meet and get to know five people well than to introduce yourself to fifty and not establish a real connection with a single one of them.

Get Phone Numbers

And when you do make these connections, take down their contact information. Preferably, phone numbers. When I meet people at an event, I usually save their contact name with the name of the event or location of the event under company so that I can easily find the person, even if I don't remember their name. And, if I am interested in further pursuing a professional relationship, my rule of thumb is to reach out within the next two days. Sometimes people might remember you even a few months later, but if the person you are trying to befriend is someone who meets a lot of different people every day, it's best to reach out as soon as possible and set up a follow-up chat or meet up. When you do reach out, over text or email, make sure you reference when and where you met them along with something specific that you connected over. It could be anything from sports to their shoes. Just something that makes your follow-up message a little more personal and lets them know that you pay attention and that you actually care.

Types of Events

The types of events you should attend vary from industry to industry. And not every networking event is branded as one. If you're smart about it, you can make any event into an event for connecting with people, because at the end of the day, that is what *every* event is meant to do: bring different people together and connect them!

The main types of networking events you can attend as a student are university events. The various departments at your university will host mixer events for students and faculty and community members who are involved with the department or the university in general.

For example, the Entrepreneurship department at my university always holds an end-of-the-year party at the

Director's house and all students involved with entrepreneurship academically or in an extracurricular fashion are invited, along with all community members who volunteered their time at the Entrepreneurship Centre. This is a great opportunity for students to meet individuals who are like-minded and truly passionate about entrepreneurship. During my time at Oxford, I attended several mixer events and one of the most memorable ones was actually held by the Mathematics, Physical, and Life Sciences (MPLS) department in conjunction with several entrepreneurship-related organisations and entities within the university structure. This was a great event that brought diverse minds together, and we were all able to share who we were and connect with people we might not have met if it weren't for that particular event. So, try to find events that will give you access to the type of people you wouldn't meet otherwise.

The Career Services department at your university will also host various recruiting events where you can meet representatives from companies that are looking to hire interns and recent graduates from your university. If you're looking to work for a company that is at one of these events, it's wise to attend and let them get to know you so that when you apply for a position, you're not just another name. They can actually put a face to your name, thus improving your chances of getting the position you are applying for!

One overlooked group of individuals who would be more than happy to talk to you and help you out is alumni! These are people who have graduated from your university and understand exactly what it's like to be a student there. If they had a wonderful time there, they would want to make sure that you enjoy the same experience and if they did not like their time at your university, they are likely to want to help you not have the same experience. Either way, it's a win-win for you! You can find alumni on social media, especially LinkedIn and at various alumni associations' events at your university. Try to establish commonalities between their experience and yours in order to start off a good relationship.

Finally, another great networking opportunity is through student organisation meetings at your university. While we talked in detail about the importance of being involved with student clubs and organisations, what we didn't touch on was the professional element of it. There will be many different clubs and organisations that are professional and will bring in different speakers. Sometimes, these organisations are student organisation versions of real life organisations like the American Marketing Association or UNICEF. The guest speakers they bring in are people in the industry or sector who are experts in their fields. Getting to know these individuals and connecting with them will give you massive leverage when you're trying to find opportunities in the same field. And the best part is, they will be more than happy to help you because they will already view you as being proactive and motivated!

Other than university affiliated events, you can also attend social events in the local community which are connected to your field of study or interest. One of the biggest community events in Tampa in 2017 was the Millennial Impact Forum hosted by my friend Andrew's company, and it was an incredible opportunity for students from the universities in Tampa to come and hear the stories of leading Tampa Bay visionaries and change agents. All of them were available to chat with after and were keen to do so, because people who are creating impact want to help other people do so as well. This event was not for students exclusively, and in fact, there were many more real people than university students there, but for the students that did attend, it was a fantastic opportunity to mingle with the best of Tampa Bay's change agent community.

I would really like your biggest take away from this chapter to be the importance of having a networker's mindset. If you focus on making new friends and building real relationships, you will succeed in creating a massive network with worthy individuals. Be sure to keep it diverse in terms of the backgrounds and industries as well as ages and sexes of the people in your network. As long as your goal is meeting people, the place doesn't matter. Especially when you are starting out on your professional journey as a student.

Chapter 17

LAUNCHING YOUR CAREER

Creating an All-Star LinkedIn Profile

The first step to being successful on LinkedIn is to create a LinkedIn account. So, if you don't have one yet, please go create one. Nothing in this chapter will make sense to you until you do so. I'm waiting. GO!

Great! Now that you have a LinkedIn account, we can talk about how you can have an *awesome* LinkedIn account. I absolutely love LinkedIn and it has created some really cool opportunities for me.

Let's start with your visual appeal on LinkedIn. Most people I've talked to about LinkedIn say that your profile photo should be a professional headshot. I personally have an action photo of me giving a talk, but that's because I'm involved with speaking and want people to be able to visualise me speaking in the very second they come across my profile. So, your two best bets would be, either a professional headshot or an action shot related to your field.

The next visual element is the cover photo. For this one, you can add something that is either a background of your city, a quote, or something else that adds to your credibility.

The next thing to focus on is your headline. Your headline should be succinct yet have enough information that people will want to read your summary to know more. A common headline for students is, "Student at University of XYZ," but I personally think you should be more specific than that. You can add your major to that and any official position or topic you have experience in where you can back up the claim. Mine used to be, "International Speaker | Social Entrepreneur | International Relations Researcher" and all three of these were very accurate for what I was doing and planning to do at the time.

Your headline serves as an introduction to the summary. This summary must also be succinct and clearly outline your academic and professional background and future aspirations. Talk about your degree and what you plan to do with it. Talk about which industry you want to be a part of and why. Talk about some soft skills and how they help you in your work. Present yourself as a passionate, motivated, and driven individual by describing yourself instead of simply using those words.

Just like the headline is a teaser to get someone interested in reading your summary, the summary is a teaser to get someone interested in reading the rest of your profile. As a college student, make sure to highlight your education and your involvement on and off campus. After talking to several people, I have concluded that the best way to highlight your involvement is to summarise it under Activities and Societies under Education, but then creating separate experiences under Experience and diving deep into the most relevant and important ones. Make sure you provide as much detail as possible in your experiences. Following the same method that you used for the bullet points on your résumé is a good play. You can also add your experiences as a volunteer under the Volunteer Experience section. There's even an option to select what type of cause it's for and that helps to let people know which causes you are most passionate about, helping you unlock potential opportunities in that area.

Another important section is Skills and you must add as many relevant skills as you can, so you can gain credibility in them. A great way of getting more people to endorse you is to simply endorse other people and pray they are just as nice as you and reciprocate it. Just kidding! You're a go-getter, so make sure you message your friends and let them know you're going to endorse them and ask them to do the same for you.

Finally, the Honors and Awards section can include any scholarships, prizes, awards, and honours you've received. This doesn't need to be limited to just college and can have additions from the past if they are reasonably important or relevant. Make sure to describe what the award was given for and connect it to the relevant organisation that awarded you.

Some final reminders about LinkedIn are to get a custom URL for your profile so that you can copy and paste it easily. You can even add it to your business cards, making it easier for people to find you. Additionally, you can also add links to articles, videos, and photos that may relate to any of the content on your LinkedIn profile to help you come across as even more credible. This is also a good way to showcase yourself as someone who other people are talking about, boosting your credibility even more.

How to Use LinkedIn

Now that we've covered what you need to make your LinkedIn look adequately professional, let's talk about what you need to use LinkedIn for. In essence, LinkedIn is like a more formal version of Facebook, but a more fun version of a résumé that lets you showcase yourself to the professional world. While LinkedIn is certainly not a place for your political rants (unless your work is political), emotional stories are gaining a lot of popularity on the platform. With the introduction of video, that will only increase in the future.

Writing LinkedIn articles is a different form of blogging, and because these articles are native to the platform, they are broadcast better than those posts that link to a third-party website. You can write articles about topics that interest you and that you know enough about.

Connecting with LinkedIn

LinkedIn is actually where I first connected with my mentor, Jeff. I'd heard of him quite a bit, because he is quite involved with my university and the community but most importantly because his restaurant group owns some of the yummiest places in the popular SoHo district of Tampa. We had never met in person but one day, he probably accidentally sent me a request but I was so surprised on seeing it that I messaged him as soon as I accepted. I asked if we could meet up to chat, no agenda whatsoever. Sending that message is one of the best things I've ever done for myself and it has sparked an incredible friendship as well as mentor-mentee relationship. And, I have LinkedIn to thank for that!

Another incredible person I met through LinkedIn is my friend Siddharth. This friendship and professional relationship was also made possible with LinkedIn's help. I saw a post on my timeline asking for people to apply to be part of an initiative that would focus on furthering the United

Nations Sustainable Development Goals. Through that, I was able to connect with him and individuals all over the world and be part of an incredible cause.

Lastly, during my time as Campus Director for Hult Prize at the University of Oxford, I reached out to so many people all over the United Kingdom who were working for Tesla because I wanted to invite Elon Musk as a judge. While that didn't pan out, I was able to foster some great relationships and talk to people who were passionate about making real positive impact. In fact, for the judges that I did have at the Finals, two of the five were individuals I reached out to via LinkedIn.

So, my top tip for connecting with people on LinkedIn is to use your desktop, because it will ask you to add a note which is a short personal message, while sending out your request, or to remember to do it anyway if you are using the app version on your phone. Another tip is to engage with the posts that are on your timeline. LinkedIn will frequently show you posts that are by second- or third-degree connections, but someone in your connections will have engaged with that post. By following the advice I have given you about creating your profile, you should most likely be an all-star profile but make sure to fulfil any other requirements because that will increase your chances of being seen by other people on LinkedIn.

Chapter 18

FINDING YOUR DREAM JOB

Looking for a job or an internship is a very time- and energy-consuming process. The first thing to know, though, is the difference between the open and hidden job markets. The open job market refers to the published positions on advertisement boards, human resource websites, job posting websites and databases. So essentially, anywhere that you would traditionally look to when you're looking for a job. Problem is, this represents less than 30 percent of potentially available jobs.

What about the other 70+ percent, you ask? Well, that's what we would refer to as the hidden job market. This includes impending vacancies and new positions that are being created or added all the time. This is why having a great network is so important. And unfortunately, most people only focus on the open job market.

Job Search Mode

Ideally, while you're in job search mode, you'll be spending 80 percent of your time networking and 20 percent of your time filling out job applications that exactly match your profile. Another thing to know and remember is that the average job search lasts about 6 months, so start looking before you graduate. You need to dedicate time each week to your job search because looking for a job is a full-time job itself, and more likely than not, you're going to be balancing classes, your involvement, and your social life while still trying to find a job. So, just as you would set goals for anything else in your life, remember to use those same goal setting and accomplishing metrics in your job search. This can include how many people you meet, how much you research a company, how many interviews you secure, etc.

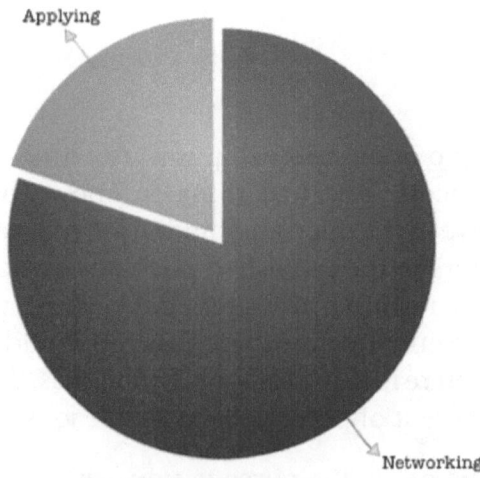

The three main activities involved in searching for a job are searching online, researching companies, and submitting the applications. These are all pretty straightforward. You can look at your university's job posting database to start. Other options include industry-specific boards, general websites, and company websites.

Company websites are great, not only to find jobs, but to excel at applying for them. By researching the values and mission of the company and gaining a sense of the work culture there, you can submit an application that is very specific and intentional which will increase your chances of getting the job you're looking for.

In terms of networking, following the guidelines in the networking chapter will help you immensely regardless of the purpose of your relationship building. Remember to always focus on the relationship building, though, and not the purpose, because you don't want to come across as desperate.

Working on Campus

On-campus jobs are awesome. In fact, they're the only jobs that work with your schedule and not vice versa. They are also very convenient because they are on campus and help you build a better network at your university. You'll be around a lot of the decision makers and higher-ups in certain offices and knowing these individuals will make your network even stronger.

The first step to having an on-campus job is to find it! We just discussed job search strategies, so implementing those for on-campus jobs will help you tremendously. Your university's database will have a list of all the openings, and sometimes you'll get emails about opportunities. Additionally, look for flyers on campus, and if you really can't find anything appealing, start talking to people at the offices and departments where you would like to work.

I got my first real on-campus job by explaining to the Director of the Entrepreneurship Centre how I spent so much of my free time at the centre anyway and that it would make sense to hire me because I already knew so much and would require little training and effort on their part. I got another one of my on-campus jobs by asking the people in that office, every week, if there was an opening. And when there was, guess who was the first person they thought of? ME! It was definitely an easier choice on their part to hire me compared to the other candidates.

On-campus jobs aren't extremely well-paid, but they will give you a little bit of spending money for the weekends, and that's a pretty good reason to have an on-campus job as a broke college student.

They can teach you new skills and even show you a passion that you may not have explored. In fact, if it weren't for my on-campus job as a Career Ambassador, this entire section wouldn't be based on facts and research. And honestly, I don't know to what extent this book would have even come to be if it weren't for that job, because it showed me how much I enjoyed helping other students succeed!

Finally, it's a great résumé builder that you can leverage to show future employers that you are well-rounded and have the necessary skills to be a professional in the real world.

Internships

My favourite thing about internships is that not only do they teach you what you enjoy, but more importantly, they also teach you what you absolutely never want to do again in your life! If you're eligible to work in the country where you are studying, do as many internships as possible, inside and outside of your field. Unfortunately, international students are limited in their options, because more than likely you will only be allowed to do internships within your field—especially in the United States. And of course, not every opportunity will be paid, and that's all right. When you're just starting out, you have to accept that you will be expected to work for free or for "academic credit" only.

Internships are beneficial in so many ways. Yes, they teach you about the field and show you what a typical day-to-day work life looks like for that field but beyond that, they help you increase your general awareness. That may be about professionalism, communication, relationship building, et cetera, and building your network even further. This is why I strongly suggest doing them for fun and for all the other benefits that they bring and not just for the academic credit and the pay. Look at those as the bonus; not the main reasons. Being an intern is a great way to learn about how the real-world tackles problems that may be mentioned in your textbooks.

Often, the current education system will not teach you about current solutions that are being employed tirelessly to solve our problems, and internships can help you learn that. Additionally, if you have real-world experience from your time at university, you're more likely to get a high-paying job after graduation. And if you want to be an entrepreneur, you would then have a great resource and network that will help you make your dream become reality.

And as an international student, or even not, you can always volunteer your time and help out companies that you may want to be involved with but cannot or do not want to officially work for. This is much easier to do with startups and small businesses, and much harder with the corporate world, but if you can leverage the other things that this book teaches you about professional development, you can certainly make things happen for yourself where most people would not be able to.

Leverage Your University into the Community

One way to double-dip and expand your involvement is to be involved with organisations with a larger reach. This can mean being a part of the campus chapter of a larger national or global organisation or becoming part of community organisations that have a presence nationally and/or globally. I know this may sound a little confusing, so here are examples of organisations that I was part of that fit these criteria.

The ONE Campaign is a global non-profit focused on eradicating extreme poverty. ONE has over 9 million members worldwide, as of March 2018, and its membership is growing daily. I first heard about this organisation through an active member of the Tampa chapter of the organisation and I was so interested in the cause that I knew I wanted to be involved. I touched on this in Part 2, when I talked about being a founding member of the ONE chapter at the University of Tampa, but the awesome part about this organisation is how many people I've been able to meet from all over the United States and the world!

I was able to stay involved with the organisation when I was studying abroad in England because one of their headquarters is in London. And, when I first went to London, I was able to tour the London office because, in 2017, I met one of the staffers at our annual conference. During the ONE Power Summit in 2018, which is the annual conference, I was able to spend some time with high-level executives in the organisation during a TV interview that I was selected to do. None of these opportunities would have come about if I hadn't been involved with setting up the campus chapter and therefore, I would really press on you, the importance of being involved with organisations like the ONE Campaign which have an incredible reach.

Off campus, my involvement with Tampa Bay's Startup Week and Startup Weekend events also allowed me to engage with individuals all over the country and the world because these are events that take place all around the world! I've been able to connect with so many people who are as passionate as I am about building great startup ecosystems in their communities.

The biggest benefit of being involved with such organisations or initiatives is the immediate network it exposes you to and the fact that it gives you a direct common passion with incredible people who are clearly interested in the same things as you. And if they are passionate change-makers in their fields and you are interested in connecting with them, they will more than likely be able to help you with whatever you may need.

Connecting with a Mentor

This is one of my favourite topics to talk about because there are so many misconceptions about mentors.

First and foremost, your mentor does *not* have to be someone who has 30 years on you. He or she does not have to be a stranger. And, while it may help in some cases, he or she does not have to be a multimillionaire.

Your mentor can be a peer, a family member, or even a friend. The role of a mentor is to guide you and be your sounding board. If you have that type of a relationship with a friend or a parent or anyone else in your life, they are a mentor to you.

This doesn't mean you can't go out and find one because, trust me, I suggest that anyway; it's just to say that you don't *need* to go out and find one when you already have people like that in your life. My mentor, Jeff, is a man in the restaurant business and other cool ventures with a great family life and a purpose-driven social entrepreneurship mindset. On paper, we may only have the last thing on that list in common but in reality, we have the best possible mentor-mentee relationship I could have asked for. When it comes to academics, I have a friend with a Ph.D. in Political Science who is my "mentor." When it comes to social entrepreneurship, I have many friends in that realm that I go to with questions and they are my "mentors." When it comes to speaking, I have a friend with 30 years of experience as a professional speaker who serves as a "mentor." In financial matters, I have another friend who answers my questions, guides me, and is like a "mentor." When it comes to relationships…

You get the point. You can have as many mentors as you want for different areas of your life. Someone once told me that they spent the majority of their 20s looking for the ideal mentor and finally realised when they were 35 that the ideal mentor doesn't exist, that instead, you can learn from and have great mentor-mentee relationships with people from different walks of life. The key is to find someone you trust, who is always looking out for you so that you can be sure that their advice comes from a genuine place.

If you do want to find a mentor, though, there are different ways to do so. Just like with networking, reaching out to people is key. If there is a specific person you want as a mentor, reach out to them via your network or LinkedIn, or find an event they will be attending and get in front of them. A friend in his 40s who is now very successful told me that the one thing he'd go back and tell his 20-year-old self is to not be intimidated by successful people.

I touched on being memorable in the chapter about references and I would like to bring it up again. If you're a 20-something-year-old, hanging out with 40-something-year-olds without being intimidated, you *will* be memorable. If you believe that you are worth it and that you belong in the same room and at the same table as them, that energy and mindset will transfer to them and you will be taken seriously. My typical friend in Tampa is a successful entrepreneur over the age of 35, and while I'm eternally grateful that they choose to spend their time with me, I also believe that I'm worth their time.

The biggest misconception about mentorships is that it's a one-way street, but in fact, the best mentor-mentee relationships are two-way streets where you can both learn from each other. My mentor tells me that he had no idea what social entrepreneurship was before he met me, even though he's technically had that mindset since before he met me. You have to bring some value to the table.

Obviously, you're seeking them as mentors because they are experts, but you have to inspire them in some way or another. Successful people are very careful about who they spend their time with, and they keep their tribe small. If you're trying to become part of someone's tribe, you have to be willing to work hard and show them that not only do you have great potential, but that you're actualising it and could do even better with their guidance.

And the best way to keep your mentors happy is by taking their advice and implementing it; and when things do work out, giving credit where it's due. I'm the first to admit that I wouldn't be where I am if it weren't for other people's belief in me and my potential. I always express gratitude to the people who help me, personally and publicly. And that makes them feel good and want to help me even more. And so I'd like to take this moment to once again thank Jeff for being an incredible mentor in my life and for everything he has and continues to do for me.

Conferences

If you're thinking of graduate school, attending and participating in conferences is one of the best things you can do for yourself.

I personally believe you should attend conferences in your field as well as those that are in fields of interest to you, even if you are not pursuing them actively. I say this because it will teach you so much about the subject and can even show you that you're passionate about something completely different from what you're pursuing. It also portrays you as a more well-rounded individual and helps you meet other people you might never have been able to meet if it weren't for that conference.

Given that I was a Political Science major, it was certainly out of my field to attend entrepreneurship conferences, but I did it anyway and this led me to meet some really cool entrepreneurs and reaffirm my belief that I wanted to be an entrepreneur, myself.

As for field-specific conferences, attending is a great way to get involved with the academic community, but what will really put you in the best light is to present your research. Different conferences have different styles of presenting options and one of the most popular conferences for students is giving a poster presentation.

Obviously, in order to be able to apply and present, you need to have conducted independent research, but posters are usually much more lax than other types of presentations and will allow you to meet faculty from across the country (if it's a bigger conference) or from across the state (if it's a smaller conference).

In fact, I'm currently on my way to a podcasting conference as I write this, and that just goes to show that attending conferences beyond your major is not just something I preach, but also practice.

Another thing to look out for when it comes to conferences, is whether your university hosts any. Most universities have some sort of conference where students can present their own research.

For students, a big hurdle with attending conferences is the monetary cost. Between conference registration fees and hotel and travel costs, you can easily shell out $1,000 and that is a *lot* for us. I know for a fact that I wouldn't have been able to attend the conferences I've attended if it weren't for grants through my university and sometimes through the conference itself. Even the conference I'm on my way to right now, Podfest, awarded me a grant to attend and my only cost was $50 for a travel accommodation that I'm sharing with a few friends and $15 for a bus from Tampa to Orlando.

There are many ways to apply for grants, but in terms of university options, let me tell you of a few options that have worked for me. Last year, I wanted to attend and present my research at multiple conferences and I knew that I couldn't afford it. So, I applied to my department, my college, and the Honors Program for grants. Between all three of those avenues, I was able to present at the Midwest Political Science Association's annual conference in Chicago as well as the Florida Political Science Association's annual conference in Orlando. There were application forms for each and they required me to submit my proposal.

The best way to get these grants is to present at the conference, not just attend. It makes the university want to invest in you, because, at the end of the day, you are not only representing yourself, but also the university. And you can always reduce your travel costs by sharing rooms with friends or other attendees and not going out to extremely expensive places for your meals.

Conferences have not only given me great exposure to the real world and the academic world, but also resulted in some great friendships.

PSA FOR INTERNATIONAL STUDENTS

■

Being an international student at a university is an incredible experience, itself. You learn so much about different cultures and get the opportunity to share yours with people who are genuinely curious and fascinated by your background. Studying at a university with a diverse population teaches you so much about the world and about different cultures, mindsets, belief systems etc.

One downside, though, is that sometimes you can feel left out. Whether that's when your friends, who are from the same country as your university, talk about childhood shows that you've never heard of or when they don't understand what you're saying when you refer to something with a name that's unfamiliar to them. While these experiences are common, each one of them is a new learning opportunity—for you and for them.

Where it gets tricky as an international student, though, is when you're looking for internships or jobs, or if you get into severe legal trouble. Please remember that this is a general overview and that your direct advisors are your best guides.

Let's dive deep into internships!

The first thing to remember is that as an international student, you can only do internships for academic credit. Legally, the American government requires you to apply for CPT (Curricular Practical Training) when you want to do any type of internship. As I mentioned, a caveat under this is that, whether it's paid or unpaid, it has to be for academic credit.

So how do you find an internship? Go back to the Job/Internship Search chapter to aid your search process. However, once you have an offer, come back here and read more.

There are three or four key individuals or offices that you'll need to talk to when it comes to getting your internship approved. The first is the Office of Career Services. They need to determine whether or not the company is legitimate and will be a safe and secure environment for you to work in. Most universities have large databases of employers and, more often than not, your employer is probably already going to be in the database. However, it's still a good idea to get them vetted through your Office of Career Services.

The second is your Academic Advisor. As an international student, you are only able to do internships within your major and your advisor is the best person to help you figure out how many credit hours you should be doing the internship for.

I said three or four individuals because sometimes there may also be an Internship Coordinator at your university who is another person that needs to be involved with the process. This person knows the ins and outs of your requirements and what you need to do exactly to fulfil the academic portion of your internship. Yes, there can be an academic component to your internship. For me, it was maintaining a journal, attending three meetings throughout the semester and writing reflections.

Finally, the International Programs Office also needs to be involved because they will help you with the official legal portion of this process. Each university does it a little differently, but mine required us to go through a short course on the basics of the CPT and helped fill out the form and such.

On the other end of this process, not only does the employer need to be vetted, but they also need to be assigned as your official Supervisor. This doesn't require much effort and you can fill out most of the information for them, but you will need an official point of contact for the internship for legal purposes.

If you don't want to get academic credit, nor do you wish to get paid, you may volunteer your free time with any organisation you choose to. This is not official in an academic sense and the legality of it is debatable, thus I can't officially comment on it. The process for finding such opportunities, though, is the same as the Job/Internship Search but more closely linked to networking than anything else. These can be within or outside your field. Always be careful and always be smart. Don't make any decisions that can jeopardise your future, especially if the major consequence is deportation.

CONCLUSION

This is just the start of my journey as an author and it's certainly just the start of my story as a "real person" and I hope to publish more books as I go on and learn and experience new things.

The goal of this book is to provide you with the necessary tools and strategies to create a successful university experience for yourself. The dichotomy of success being a subjective as well as an objective metric has always intrigued me. I mean, how you describe your personal success is up to you but if you were to meet someone who had a 4.0 GPA, tons of involvement and internship experience and a well-paying job or million-dollar business, all complete with a positive attitude and infectious smile, you would definitely think of that person as successful in the traditional sense.

As you embark on this journey for the next few years of your life, I want you to think of what success means to you personally and how that contrasts or compares to the traditional view of success. It can be the same or similar, or entirely different– it doesn't matter! The important part is to know what you want to get out of your time at university. The opportunities are endless but finding the right opportunities can be overwhelming and may require hard-work. Having a general idea will benefit you tremendously. And remember, I am here for you every step of the way. You can reach out to me over email or social media and I will do my best to guide you in the right direction. I don't want to say that university was the best time of my life given that I want every moment to be my best moment, but I do believe that I had the best university experience I could've possibly had and I wish the same for you. Regardless of the storms or the sunshine, always remember, YOU are greater than the highs and the lows.

I hope this book helps you with your journey as a university student because your time at university is going to be incredible. I hope my experiences and advice can give you the tools to have the best time EVER!

RESEARCH TO EXPLORE

Anderson, Matthew. "Vocational Education as a Driver of Growth in the Economy." Lecture. https://www.britishcouncil.kz/sites/default/files/3._matt_a_tvet_uk_-_british_council_astana_nov14.pdf.

Bratskeir, Kate. "You Judge People The Second You Meet Them, And They Judge You Back." HuffPost UK. April 05, 2016. https://www.huffingtonpost.co.uk/entry/judging-people-first-impression_us_56cf70f6e4b03260bf761c12?guccounter=1.

Cuddy, Amy. TED: Ideas worth Spreading. June 2012. https://www.ted.com/talks/amy_cuddy_your_body_language_shapes_who_you_are.

Support. "Eating Disorders in College Students." Child Mind Institute. August 30, 2017. https://childmind.org/article/eating-disorders-and-college/.

223D. "Education and Training." Education and Training Home. https://benefits.va.gov/GIBILL/ForeverGIBill.asp.

Global Status Report on Alcohol and Health. Report. 2011. http://www.who.int/substance_abuse/publications/global_alcohol_report/msbgsruprofiles.pdf.

"Grin and Bear It! Smiling Facilitates Stress Recovery." Association for Psychological Science. July 30, 2012. https://www.psychologicalscience.org/news/releases/smiling-facilitates-stress-recovery.html.

"How to Increase the Odds of Reaching Your Goals by 85%." Shay Goulding Meurer. May 05, 2015. https://uponly.co/2015/01/08/how-to-increase-the-odds-of-reaching-your-goals-by-85-2/.

"Know Your Rights on Campus: Sexual Harassment and Sexual Assault under Title IX." AAUW: Empowering Women Since 1881. https://www.aauw.org/what-we-do/legal-resources/know-your-rights-on-campus/campus-sexual-assault/.

Mueller, Pam A., and Daniel M. Oppenheimer. "The Pen Is Mightier Than the Keyboard." *Psychological Science* 25, no. 6 (2014): 1159-168. doi:10.1177/0956797614524581.

Novotney, Amy. "Procrastination or 'intentional Delay'?" *GradPSYCH Magazine,* January 2010. January 2010. http://www.apa.org/gradpsych/2010/01/procrastination.aspx.

Salemi, Vicki. "New Survey Shows Smiling Is Best Way to Make First Impression." – Adweek. February 26, 2013. https://www.adweek.com/digital/new-survey-shows-smiling-is-the-best-way-to-make-a-first-impression/.

"Seasonal Affective Disorder (SAD)." Life with Antisocial Personality Disorder (ASPD) | Mind, the Mental Health Charity - Help for Mental Health Problems. June 2016. https://www.mind.org.uk/information-support/types-of-mental-health-problems/seasonal-affective-disorder-sad/about-sad/#.Wz-vVbaZMWr.

"Study Finds Tens of Millions of Americans Drink Alcohol at Dangerously High Levels." National Institute on Alcohol Abuse and Alcoholism. May 17, 2017. https://www.niaaa.nih.gov/news-events/news-releases/study-finds-tens-millions-americans-drink-alcohol-dangerously-high-levels.

Weber, Lauren. "Your Résumé vs. Oblivion." The Wall Street Journal. January 24, 2012. https://www.wsj.com/articles/SB10001424052970204624204577178941034941330?-mod=e2tw.

Wormald, Benjamin. "America's Changing Religious Landscape." Pew Research Center's Religion & Public Life Project. May 12, 2015. http://www.pewforum.org/2015/05/12/americas-changing-religious-landscape/.

A big thank you to the following individuals for backing the crowdfunding campaign that helped to publish this book:

Amanda Patanow

Drew Hall

Jeff Gigante

Jim Barnish

Peter Kageyama

Topher Morrison

Walter Matthews

And a shoutout to Jimmy Clark because I am a woman of my word!

ABOUT THE AUTHOR

Juhi Kore (Ju-hee Ko-ray) was born and raised in Bombay (Mumbai), India and moved to Tampa, Florida in August 2015, for her undergraduate education. During her three years of undergrad, she also spent some time at the University of Oxford in England. Juhi majored in Political Science, with a concentration in World Affairs and minored in Leadership Studies and Urban Studies, at the University of Tampa. She successfully graduated in May 2018 with an Honors distinction and received several awards for her active citizenship and leadership initiatives in her university and local communities. Juhi has been a mentor to over 120 students during her college experience and is very passionate about helping other students create successful university experiences for themselves that will set them on a path of lifelong learning.

As an international student herself, she understands the additional hardships that come with being on the other side of the planet as one's family and is able to provide specific guidance to other students in the same position.

You can learn more about Juhi by visiting her website at www.juhikore.com or yougotthisthebook.com

www.ingramcontent.com/pod-product-compliance
Lightning Source LLC
Chambersburg PA
CBHW020411080526
44584CB00014B/1272